RATS IN THE SACRISTY

RATS IN THE SACRISTY

BY

LLEWELYN POWYS

*With fourteen wood engravings
by Gertrude M. Powys*

Essay Index Reprint Series

BOOKS FOR LIBRARIES PRESS, INC.
FREEPORT, NEW YORK

First published 1937
Reprinted 1967

LIBRARY OF CONGRESS CATALOG NUMBER:
67-30226

PRINTED IN THE UNITED STATES OF AMERICA

Allow the ear to hear what it likes, the eye
to see what it likes, the nose to smell what
it likes, the mouth to say what it likes, the
body to enjoy what it likes, and the mind
to do what it likes.—YANG CHU.

DEDICATED

TO

GEORGE SANTAYANA

PREFACE

INFORMAL and casual appreciation of great historic and legendary figures can often be, in the hands of a kindred spirit, more illuminating than the most exhaustive and erudite interpretations. Such I feel is especially true of these lively and characteristic essays of my brother.

A man of letters is known by the intellectual company he keeps; and it interests me to trace the occult affinities between these very different guests of my brother's mind, answering as they must do, for all their diversity, certain deep spontaneous demands in so devoted an adherent.

Is it possible, among such a gathering of great ones, in this very personal and private Elysian Field, to catch at some quality shared by all, which, like the brand on the back of a goodly flock, marks them as belonging to the same fold? This quality can hardly be what Nietzsche calls the "Dionysian," as against the "Apollonian," for any great teacher less "Dionysian" than Confucius could hardly be found.

But what could, I think, be said of them all is that they bring down divine philosophy to the earth and emphasize the power of the Real in human life, the Real apprehended through the Senses, *as against*

the Ideal. And this is what Llewelyn is always
looking for in his authors—a robust assertion of the
divinity of the senses as against every other
divinity !

Many of my brother's admirers, being averse—
good easy men—to the dust of controversy, have
greatly regretted his debouchings and sly sallies into
the perilous arenas of morals and religion; but,
after all, a writer's character *is* his character, and
there is something satisfying about a consistency
that, like a ram invading a fowl-run, refuses to
budge, or to cease snuffing quizzically at the
" chicken-feed," for all the indignant flutter.

Sturdily indeed does Llewelyn Powys reiterate
his obstinate conviction that things are as they
seem—bone-real, not puff-ball ideal—and that if we
are too timid to take this tough world at its face-
value we'd best cry quit and let it spin; for by
Cock and Pye we shall get no more, no ! not a stiver,
charm we never so wisely.

And what power there still is—invisible as well as
visible—in the *status quo* of established tradition !
This can be seen in the weary derision with which,
half-unconsciously perhaps, easy-going people " put
into Coventry," as the school-boys say, a writer who
can't leave well alone.

" Why doesn't Llewelyn Powys go back to his
enchanting sketches of country-life ? Why doesn't
he go back to his travels and the engaging whimsies
of his friends and relations ? Why must he tilt, like

a crotchety Don Quixote, *gone suddenly sane*—a murrain on him !—at the age-old irrationalities of Church and State ? "

For how should we not—we mumping mummers of the Unseen, the Unheard, the Untouched—wince and grow testy, when this old incorrigible Visible World that we have been at such pains to perforate with our " second thoughts " is made to loom up again, solid and ultimate as ever ?

Personally I still think there is more in life than he wots of, with his four-square visible world. Yes, for all your goats-beard poetizing of the five senses, Master, I am as certain as ever I was that the real reality lies behind it all, and that " something " in us answers to " something " outside it all.

But I know what moonshine these " somethings " of mine are to you ; and the question between us is as old as humanity. Long after we are dead this tug-of-war will still be going on ; and you may take my word for it, it will never be only the established interests, never only the proprietors and the proprieties, that will be upset by your " stamped, sealed, and delivered " sense-world !

Well, after all, it is for the way these things are written, for the humour in them and the passion and the poetry in them, that posterity will read our disputes. When I think of this I fear sometimes that the tough-minded realists like Llewelyn Powys and his robust predecessors are bound in nature to have the prevailing word. But then I console myself by remembering that neither words, nor the lively senses from which they draw their vigour, have ever yet proved themselves equal to limiting the mystery of life.

JOHN COWPER POWYS

Corwen,
   North Wales.

Grateful acknowledgment is made to the following Journals for allowing some of these essays to be reprinted : *The Aryan Path, The Bookman, John O' London's Weekly, The Nineteenth Century and After, The Rationalist Annual, The Dublin Magazine, The Saturday Review of Literature, The New York Herald Tribune, The Virginia Quarterly, The Literary Guide.*

CONTENTS

G. M. Powys.

DIONYSOS

DIONYSOS

IT is interesting to meditate upon the similarity and difference between the Christian and the Dionysian cults, between these two imaginary deities who have had so memorable an influence upon the world. Out of the fecund earth the race of men arose, rank protagonists, moon-mad, sun-begotten, their fleeting stay above ground bewildered by the violence of their emotions, by the ineffectual ratiocinations of their light brains. Their distracting predicament quickened their spirits to invent dreams of redemption.

In every land these religious interpretations have sprung up, and the figure of Jesus and the figure of Dionysos have represented centres of worship for two very significant streams of religious philosophy.

There exists a persistent legend that the mysterious Nysa, where the nymph suckled Dionysos in a cave, is actually situated on the bank of a tributary of the river Jordan, not far from the city of Beisan in Palestine. It is possible, therefore, that not only on the spiritual plane, but on the physical plane as well, by a natal chance of actual geographical proximity, these two protagonists of human liberation may be closely associated. I like to think it is so. I like to think that the wild sensitive spirit of Jesus and the wild sensitive spirit of Dionysos were both incarnate upon the same parcel of Syrian soil, that they both saw the sun rise and set over a similar landscape as they played by day; and after darkness had fallen, lay in the arms of their mothers, intent to listen to the voices of the night. Jesus shared with Dionysos the gift of prophecy, shared with him an impatience with human bigotry, and like him could upon occasions display the unpredictable temper of a God. But there the convergence of the two ends. The teaching of Jesus in its ultimate essence is more subtle, more sophisticated, more decadent, and, with all reverence be it said, more subversive to human happiness. The Apollonian ideal of moral order, of intellectual enlightenment, of sanity, has been less dangerous. Jesus, through his idealism, through the example of his personal heroism, sought to exorcise for ever the despair men feel on discovering that the grass fields of their familiar earth hide cracks and gulfs of horror. He called upon his followers to bring redemption to life by denying life, to save their souls by losing them; and not only was earth-life repudiated by him on the score of its darker secrets, but also on account of its lure " of things too sweet."

The Dionysian guidance, the Dionysian art of life, was simpler and braver. This mountain god, hailing ultimately from the far north and immediately from Thrace, taught that the recoil from lurking

terror can be resolved only by a still more abandoned
acceptance of the vital principle. The true Dionysian
spirit endeavours always to become one with the very
Yggdrasil root of existence so greatly to be feared, so
greatly to be adored. It does not attempt to under-
take the impossible task of controlling life after the
Apollonian tradition, still less does it turn aside
from life after the Christian manner. It ratifies life,
embraces life, and aims through ecstasy of worship
to become identified with the reality behind matter,
behind the shivering wave-lengths of the objective
universe; to become one with that mysterious stir
that first troubled the inanimate. In those moments
when the authentic transport, the true Dionysian
rapture has taken possession of a man, all is forgotten.
He shares with the cat the glare of her green eyes,
and with the mouse, damp with her spittle, the
ecstasy of martyrdom. Then when the madness is
over there follows in the lull, in the succeeding hush
" of the silence of the Bacchæ," the most strange,
the most precious of all religious experiences, when,
in a state of mystic quietude, the worshipper medi-
tates with imagination, with compassion, upon the
thronging irresponsible dream presented to his
senses. There exists always an undying antithesis
between the regular and the irregular, between the
ordered and the disordered; and, although in practice
it is incumbent upon all civil spirits to engage in the
hopeless struggle against stupidity, injustice, and
cruelty, we can still preserve with edification an area

of secret conviction, an area of personal affirmation
of the more oblique, the more implacable metaphysic.

Whenever we separate ourselves from Nature we
do so at our peril. The restrictions, however
necessary they may be, imposed upon our free
happiness by society are in themselves pernicious,
and when we add to them the gratuitous restraints
of ascetic persuasions, the health, the generosity of
the strongest soul is in jeopardy. Any inordinate
forcing of selflessness defeats its own end, for a stage
is reached when the outraged person will turn upon
himself, upon others. In the religion of Dionysos
this tension finds relief. When the satyr train left
" their brooms and cold mushrooms "; when the
Bacchæ, thyrsus in hand, danced with heads thrown
back; when the wise Silenus was on his " gaping "
ass behind the triumphant leopard-drawn chariot,
civilized ceremony was annulled, discounted under a
blithe amoral dispensation. Once more the flood-
gates of Nature were open and the world was happy.
It was not for nothing that the ancients named
India as the country of this God's most important
conquest, India that more than any other land has
harboured thoughts recreant to the sun.

At any moment a Dionysian neophyte may, in a
state of exultant consciousness, be in communion
with the vital leap which exists beyond and below all
human commitments. Yesterday as I came along a
lane in April sunshine I experienced the perennial
thrill. It came to me with so common a spectacle

as nettles growing in the ditch and smelling rough in
the new heat of the spring, of nettles unknown in
heaven, thrusting themselves up through the cow
parsley with all the wilful assurance of the vegetable
world at the approach of a new season.

Dionysos was essentially a vegetable God. His
life, they used to say, was in " the sap and bark ";
and in our time his unstable influence is still suggested
by the more wanton growths of the open country,
by the sprawling trailer of the blackberry, by the
vigour of the throttling ivy, and by the gnarled and
contorted vine-stump out of which the images and
idols of the God—so Walter Pater declared—used to
be carved. These vegetable growths, then, are his
most apparent symbols, suggesting the bountiful
aspect of his religion that leads our minds to a
comprehensive acceptance of a condition of intense
poetic sensibility which recognizes as sacramental
the plain food of our nourishment—brown meat,
yellow honey, bread, and, above all, wine.

It would seem that intoxication was not used by
his followers as a substitute in the Freudian sense,
but rather as a positive instrument of grace through
the use of which life could be experienced more
abundantly, the manifestations of the physical world
being then seen through " divine eyeballs." We have
here the highest reward of the Dionysian mood, the
power it can exert to stir men out of their congenital
lethargy, out of their gross habit of accepting
existence with unillumined minds. Such lumpish-

ness is not possible to those who follow in the train of
" mad Dionysos " and his nurses, who follow in the
train of him " who lives in the tree." For, as that
man of many mischiefs, Plato, said, " the madness
sent by God is better than the moderation of men."
No higher function is possible to religion than to
evoke a transported contemplation of the mystery of
existence here on earth. During these inspired states
dolour is dissipated, our petty preoccupations van-
quished. True religion derives directly from the
sense of awe natural in man at his first wakening to
consciousness. " Shall things of dust the God's
dark ways despise ? "

There is a valuable secret in this orgiastic tradition.
Civilized society has not been satisfied with the
success it has had in subjecting our individual desires
to its service, but, still apprehensive, it deliberately
disparages sensuality, wilfully coercing the carnal
urge towards its ideal of submissive domesticity.
With this consummation of man's life decried it is
small wonder that the faces in our streets are care-
worn and bitter, so that it has come to seem almost a
mockery to mention this deity of the grape-cluster.
The Dionysian spirit gives its sanction to every
declaration of freedom, it stands in stubborn opposi-
tion to theories of idealistic teaching. Whenever
two or three are gathered together in happiness,
there is present the God-like figure of Dionysos.
He is the deity who brings to man the greatest
wisdom, teaching him to turn back to natural joys

and with a free mind to drink, to laugh, to dance. What can we do better than to cast ourselves before this great Nature-God, accepting the cruelty and ugliness as inseparable from life, recognizing their intrusion with a level eye, and yet continuing our laudations with an infatuated trust? There is no more deadly enemy of the lust for aggression, for empire, than the Dionysian compassion, the Dionysian happiness, the Dionysian generosity and strength. This Dasyllios, the dweller in the thickets, this Agrionios, the ruthless one, puts us into a state to accept the riot of the visible. With our sight purged by his exultation we experience God-like excitement from the simplest spectacle—from the crafty physiognomy of an owl peering down at us from its beam stool, from the flickering butterflies!

To meditate upon the handiwork of the Sun, "whom men call Dionysos," we can do nothing better. There is no cry that approximates more nearly to the voice of the earth than the "goat cry" of this suffering and debonnaire God. From the forests it rises, from the vineyards, from the rustling cornfields, reaching to the farthest stars whose light has turned red with age. "O Dionysos, in no wise endured by mortals." It is a cry charged with thought beyond the scrupulous reason, with thought commingled with the senses, with the more errant emotions, the cry of the planet, explicit of terror, explicit of ecstasy. How in the height of summer, at the time of the solstice, the thick hayfields, the tangled hedges—the most inconspicuous meadow-corner decked as for a gala—put us in mind of this ancient adoration, fill us with the assurance that Dionysos will come again, will return to earth once more with his fox-maidens swarming about his triumphal car! To surrender ourselves utterly to a consciousness that surpasses consciousness—this is our largest release. It is a religion that can never die. It has in it a solace for the yearning of the human heart. For this reason it was strong enough to force its acceptance upon the temperate Greeks. At first the Hellenic mind found difficulty in assimilating its wild rout. Eventually, however, it came to share equal honours with the cult of Apollo, as is proved by the huge stone at Delphi with these words carved upon it : " Here lieth the body of Dionysos the son of Semele." It was an example of sacerdotal roguery of the simpler and nobler sort; though, whether regarded in the light of fact or of allegory, it remained none the less a deceit to be discredited. The truth of it is that Dionysos, with his race of " worthless, idle satyrs," can never die.

> " By his own joy I vow
> By the grape upon the bough."

This faith lies below Christianity, below science. It is as much opposed to transcendental values as it is to matter-of-fact values. Always it draws its indestructible power from the senses. It claims the glory of life to be revealed by the flesh of man. In the face of all ultimate issues it is sceptical, disillusioned. At the best our difficult compromises are inconsequently ephemeral, comparable to the thriftless applications of gnats, which, doomed instantly to an ignominious extinction, whirl through a twilight air above a swiftly flowing river without dykes or weirs. What has happened to all those heroic causes of the past for which so much human blood has been shed, and for the achievement of which so much human passion has been expended? Magnanimities, despicable villainies, all swept away, all forgotten! The evening of the crucifixion did not stay for one single second the untiring procedure of manifold Nature.   The hyæna, with hindquarters slouched, came slinking that night over the dusty hillside to sniff after the buried yellow bones of a punctilious Pharisee; the mangered Palm Sunday ass stopped her braying on the Mount of Olives as, with a single intention, she turned her grey head towards the heap of fodder thrown into the dusty corner of her shed. On a battle-field where a thousand men lie mutilated, the dandelions and buttercups patiently, punctually, close their petals at the going down of the sun. The basic structure of earth-life is subject to an appalling precipitation. The religion of Dionysos accepts this fact, makes no pretence that it is otherwise.   Its votaries are content to celebrate existence without exacting reservations, to worship the unthinking omnipotent force with inebriate fervour as the red sap of confident life pours through their veins.

If once we have given ourselves to this redeemed vision, then we can afford to tamper with our pre-concerted moralities. For every day through our windows we shall hear the unmistakable cry strengthening our infirm bodies, dispelling our ghostly mistrusts, and forcing us to acknowledge the triumph of disobedient life. In so far as we succeed in impressing each one of our experiences with the Dionysian spirit, we shall be happy. As young men, as old men, to acclaim the glory of life with un-grudging senses, this is the ultimate loyalty.

G. M. Powys.

AKHENATON, THE SUN-WORSHIPPER

AKHENATON, THE SUN-WORSHIPPER

" Still we hear it—
Clear, immortal, undying—
The old sweet chant
Of those who worship the sun ! "

YESTERDAY I unearthed a remarkable ammonite in a Dorset sea-coast cliff.   The noonday sun was shining bright upon the circular whorls of the fossil, the formation of which suggested that I had uncovered a ram's horn of enormous proportions which, through the passing of long geological ages, had become ossified.   Ulysses might well have escaped from the cave of Polyphemus clinging to the golden-fleeced belly of an animal whose neck had been strong enough to support such armour.   As I examined the stone with the sunlight illuminating each crevice of its surface, there came to my mind the record of an ancient war between two gods.   The name of the fossil I looked at was derived, I knew, from the Egyptian deity whose symbol was a ram's horn.

Thirty-three hundred years have gone by since Akhenaton challenged the power of the priests of Thebes, whose superstitions were especially associated with Ammon.   In early times the human race was prone to explain the inexplicable with supernatural

imaginings. As man's brain developed, separating
him farther and farther from the beasts of the field,
his unexercised intelligence followed naturally enough
the easiest and simplest paths suggested—paths of
irrational inference. To look at the mummified
skulls of the early Egyptians, so narrow, so hare-like
in shape, is to realize in a flash how inevitable was
this period of ghostly assumptions. The unexpected
intrusion of the natural worship of Akhenaton, out of
all theoretic time-sequence, is one of the most startling
happenings in the story of religious growth.

The Pharaohs of the eighteenth dynasty had come
to attribute their military success to the strong arm
of Ammon. It was, they thought, through the
roaring of Ammon, the great god of Thebes, that
Egyptian suzerainty had been advanced into the
heart of Syria. Amenhotep I had not hesitated to
appropriate to his own personal use the awful
syllables of the god's name, while Thothmes III
ascribed his military success to Ammon's partiality.

The origin of Akhenaton's revolutionary views
remains obscure. Some have suggested that his
mind was influenced by his mother, the celebrated
dowager queen, who may have had first-hand knowledge of the various cults of the Syrian Adon, or
Adonis, as he was known in Greece; others would
have us believe that the new faith was at first a mere
matter of statecraft, by means of which the young
Pharaoh hoped to free the throne from the irksome
thraldom of an exacting hierarchy. Those of us,

however, who read with understanding the religious sayings of the epoch, will soon become convinced that this interlude of philosophic monotheism, born out of due time, owed its existence above everything to the spiritual genius of this most interesting and original of all the Pharaohs. " The words of Ra are before me. . . . My august father (God) taught me their essence and revealed them to me. . . . They were known in my heart, opened to my face. I understood." The death-mask of Akhenaton confirms this, the withered shell of his countenance being eloquent still of his soul's profound yearning. Indeed, it was his sensitive response to religious feeling, in its deeper and more refined aspects, which caused him to recoil so violently from the crude conceptions prevailing in Egypt—prevailing in that ancient nest out of which all priestly tribes of the world have sprung.

Akhenaton found it incredible that the secret of life could centre about a God of terrible judgments, a God of war. This " great one of visions," with the quick insight of a prophet, sought the Deity on a more spiritual plane, sought him in the reality behind reality, in that sphere " whose centre is everywhere and circumference nowhere."

Men of science to-day assure us that, if God exists, his influence is to be found in that margin of physical sub-atomic matter, which may be likened to a veritable Merlin's circle of mystery, out of the reach of man's sense observation. Akhenaton in his philosophy

found God in this area. This absolute " behind
the sun " to which he renders homage is the absolute
which we conceive behind the group-waves, behind
ultimate matter. But Akhenaton was not only a
religious prophet—he was an artist and a poet,
and in moments of inspiration he was able to see
God's shadow upon the waters of the Nile, was able
to hear his breath amid the bland flowers of his
pleasure-garden at noon. " Thy love is great and
large. Thou fillest the two lands of Egypt with Thy
love."

In a subtle manner he seems to have identified
Aton, a word ultimately derived from Adon (the
sinking sun), with Ra-Horakhti (the ancient sun-
god of Heliopolis) until the end of his reign. " The
Aton " stood alone as the one and only God for
whom the disc of the sun was taken as the outward
and visible sign. Akhenaton was the first man to
apprehend the immortal secret that God is where
poetry is; is present in the rustling leaves of amorous
date-palms; is present in the depths of tropical
oceans, where unnamed fish seek for their meat with
blank, patient stare; is present with the calf as it
frolics in a field of scarlet poppies; is confederate
with the light-waves of the farthest nebulæ beyond
our own island universe.

So inimical were the Theban priests, and so sottish
were the common people to his new religion, that
Akhenaton took the drastic and dramatic step of
abandoning the capital city and founding another

royal city, " The City of the Horizon of Aton,"
farther up the Nile, some hundred and sixty miles
above where the city of Cairo now stands.

There, in a lovely valley on the eastern bank of the
great stream, protected by high escarpments, temple,
palace, and villa rose up to the glory of Aton. In
this happy holiday city, the old sacerdotal, necro-
philiastic beliefs were largely superseded, and men
and women, boys and girls, were taught, with minds
free and bodies free, to worship the creative force in
spirit and in truth. The new temples were con-
structed with altars open to the sunshine, and upon
these altars sacrifices were made without bloodshed;
vegetables, fruit, and flowers being substituted for
animal, for human flesh. In his decorations Akhenaton introduced a completely new form of art, a
strange art, spontaneous and at the same time
archaic; while for the first time in the history of
Egypt a Pharaoh is portrayed moving freely among
his people. A twilight hour had fallen upon Ammon.
Peace and goodwill towards men had come to Egypt.
And it is to be noticed that in the frescoes the
" prisoner and captives " are no longer being
despitefully treated.

> " O tremulous hope ! O large escape
> From the intolerable oppressors !
> O bent and bowed resume your shape,
> And dispossess the dispossessors."

From various sources we gather that the population of the City of the Horizon passed its hours in a

manner at once simple and sophisticated. There is
a butterfly delicacy about the life of this Utopia of
antiquity that has never been equalled. " There is
no poverty for him who has set thee, Oh ! Aton, in
his heart. It is impossible for such a one to say
' Oh ! that I had.' " Always we see Akhenaton,
this young intellectual Pharaoh, represented under
a halo of physical and spiritual grace In happy
guise we see him driving abroad in his chariot with
Nefertiti, his darling, his heart's root, at his side.
Carelessly he curbs his two mettlesome horses, while
she lifts her head to kiss his lips as a bird might
flutter before settling upon an overhanging bough.
We see him reclining at a feast, the table heaped with
fruit and flowers, and his little handmaid daughters,
so precious to him, standing by with pretty offerings.
It is small wonder his oath of favourite use was " As
my heart is happy in the Queen and her children,"
or that he alluded to Nefertiti as " Mistress of my
happiness at hearing whose voice the King rejoices."
All the harsh values of the world were reversed in
this favoured city, beauty and happiness being
recognized as the twin aims of life. On every side
the refined æsthetic tastes of the King were reflected :
in the decorative cobras carved on the lintels of his
airy halls, in the lotus flowers about the capitals of
the tall columns, in the coloured ostrich-plumed
standards, in the very paving-stones, so warm to a
naked foot, where wild-fowl were pictured disturbing
the marsh insects as they rose out of the rushes.

" So six long years he revell'd, night and day,
  And when the mirth wax'd loudest, with dull sound
  Sometimes from the grove's centre echoes came,
  To tell his wondering people of their king,
  In the still night, across the steaming flats,
  Mix'd with the murmur of the moving Nile."

More than ever confident of his new religion,
Akhenaton now made an attempt to eradicate out of
the land the very memory of Aton's rival, the dreaded
Ammon-Ra of Thebes. His couriers and officials
were instructed to make an exhaustive search through
every town and village for the purpose of erasing all
signs and symbols of the hated name. A decree
had gone forth from the Glory of Aton that the God
Ammon " should die and not live." So thorough
were the messengers that they travelled into the
farthest deserts, and wherever the word " Ammon "
appeared on rock or quarry wall it was effaced. They
even ventured to open royal tombs, and were not
content until the baleful letters had been obliterated
from the tiniest funeral ornament. All memory of
this King of the Gods was to be removed, and even
from the name of his own father, Akhenaton did not
hesitate to strike out the hated syllables.

The worship of Akhenaton, this " Son of the Sun "
as he delighted to call himself, consisted in the conscious adoration of the mysterious force that sustains
not only the shadows of flesh that are men, but the
whole riot of the objective universe. The symbol of
the sun's disc was represented as shedding down the
beneficent " heat which-is-in-Aton " upon mortal

life, upon animal life, upon bird life, upon fish life, and upon insect life, each ray being limned with a diminutive hand of benediction. It was a religion uncontaminated, exacting no other obligation than a disposition of worship before the unfathomable secrets of existence. " Thou art alone, but infinite vitalities are in Thee by means of which to give life to Thy creatures." The hours of dawn and of sunset were set apart for prayer. It was then that the " beauties " of the Aton were most apparent, and it is at those hours that human beings are most susceptible to the influence of sublimity. To Akhenaton and his followers " living in truth " the power behind the Aton was " Lord of Fate, Origin of Fate and of Chance which gives life." How the words of this man come down to us from that remote time, having still upon them the stamp of his mind, simple, sincere, and deeply poetical. " This beautiful child of Aton " gives us the clue to an honourable religion. Utterances of pure gold are upon his lips, upon the lips of this " Lord of Sweetness "—a title often to be found inscribed on the backs of the scarabs of his period.

It was the influence of the Aton that caused " the food and fatness of Egypt." It was the Aton which was " a witness of that which pertains to eternity . . . the remembrancer of eternity." It was the sun that symbolized the intangible, ineffable spirit present everywhere throughout the objective substance of matter, the procreant urge that had created " flesh, bones, and all things that have to do with the per-

fection of man's nature." It was the same omnipotent influence, made manifest in Ra, which " had
brought up millions by its bounty. All that thou
hast made," cried Akhenaton, " leaps before thee !
. . . It is life to see Him, there is death in not seeing
Him."

Of all the hymns of praise that human tongues
have chanted from the cornlands of the earth, few
can compare to Akhenaton's chant preserved to us
in stiff hieroglyphics. Out of the dust men have
risen—animals of wit, prevision, and feeling—
and in spite of taloned fingers and hairy scalps, they
have been found capable of celebrating with mouths
of clay the Glory of Life. The universe under its
primal discipline, with heavy atoms and light atoms
as much active in the eye of the sovereign serpent as
in the remotest star-cloud, has cast up thought, and
from the curved lips of intelligence there rises a
pæan of worship as moving as the sound of the sea,
as charmed as wind in a forest. It is as though mind
sang to mind, matter to matter, the sun to the sun :—

> " Thy rising is beautiful in the horizon of
> heaven. O thou Aton, who hadst thine existence
> in primeval times. When thou risest in the
> eastern horizon thou fillest every land with thy
> beauties. Thou art beautiful to see, and art
> great, and art like crystal, and art high above the
> earth. . . . Thou art remote, but thy beams are
> upon the earth. . . . So long as thou art in the
> heavens day shall follow thy footsteps. When
> thou settest in the western horizon the earth is
> in darkness and is like a being that is dead.

Men lie down and sleep in their habitations,
their heads are covered up, and their nostrils
stopped and no man can see his neighbour. . . .
When thou risest in the horizon the earth
lightens, and when thy beams shine forth it is
day. . . . Over all the earth men perform their
work. All beasts and cattle repose in their
pastures, and the trees and the green herb put
forth their leaves and flowers. The birds fly
out of their nests and their wings praise thee as
they fly forth. . . . The boats float down and
sail up the river likewise, for thy path is opened
when thou risest. The fish in the stream leap
up towards thy face, and thy beams shine through
the waters of the great sea. Thou makest male
seed to enter into women, and thou causest the
liquid seed to become a human being. Thou
makest the man-child to live in the body of his
mother. Thou makest him to keep silent so
that he cry not, and thou art a nurse to him in
the womb.
. . . When the chicken is in the egg, and is
making a sound within the shell, thou givest it
air inside it so that it may keep alive. Thou
bringest it to perfection so that it may split the
egg shell. How manifold are thy works ! They
are hidden from before us, O thou sole God,
whose power no other possesseth. Thou didst
create the earth according to thy desire, while
thou wast alone : men, all cattle large and
small, that are upon the earth, that go upon
their feet, all that are on high, that fly with their
wings, the countries of Syria and Nubia, and
the land of Egypt."

This enlightened religion lasted but a brief space.
Akhenaton died about the year 1358 B.C., when he
was still a young man, and even before his death had

been strictly taught that the rough world was unripe for his innocent cult.   His pacific persuasions squared ill with his age.   Greed and lust for power—what consideration were they likely to show to so civilized a Prince, whose chief delight lay in religion and whose principal happiness was involved in his beautiful Nefertiti, "who sends the Aton to rest with a sweet voice, and with her two beautiful hands bearing two systrums"?   All Syria was soon in rebellion, and disaster followed disaster.

Akhenaton, it seems, died suddenly, perhaps of epilepsy.   It was now the turn of the priests for revenge.   From every monument the new word " Aton " was erased.   They too visited the necropolis and broke into the tomb of Akhenaton, into the tomb of " that criminal," as he was now referred to in documents of state.   Fortunately they omitted to deface the death inscription on the coffin :   " The Beautiful Prince, the chosen one of Ra, the King of upper and lower Egypt, living in Truth, Lord of the Two Lands, Akhenaton, the beautiful child of the living Aton, whose name shall live for ever and for ever."

G. M. Powys.

CONFUCIUS

CONFUCIUS

K'UNG FUTZE, the philosopher K'ung, or, in its Latinized form, Confucius, was born some eight hundred years after the death of Akhenaton, the Egyptian sun-worshipping Pharaoh. During his span of life the battle of Marathon was fought, the Jews returned from their captivity and rebuilt their temple at Jerusalem, Lars Porsena failed to reinstate the Tarquins at Rome, and the early inhabitants of Britain, with stag-horns for picks and the shoulder-blades of oxen for shovels, were engaged in raising earthworks.

The civilization of China is of such extreme antiquity, and the spiritual and mental orientations of the Mongolian races are so different from our own, that it is hard to estimate the position that Confucius takes as a world teacher. Probably no Western mind has ever appreciated him at his true worth; indeed, it is perhaps possible for us only to guess at the significance he has for the yellow races, more numerous than flies.

The Chinese, with their quaint jigsaw minds, childish, but at the same time extremely profound, have never been distinguished for what is known to us as " a religious sense." The references to God con-

tained in their ancient books—in the Yi-King and
Shu-King, for instance—are so light that they could
never have been responsible for the gloomy fanaticism
that we associate with such cities as Thebes, Babylon,
Jerusalem, or Mecca. By these practical rice-
cultivators, who used to believe that the earth was
square, the day-by-day manners of a man are regarded as being of much more consequence than his
opinions.

These Chinese, with heads like pots of yellow clay,
have never rated the faculty of faith very high, and
for the most part have no knowledge of those mystical
intimations out of which our metaphysical idealism arises. With regard to supernatural matters,
the cultivated classes have remained throughout the
generations ironically sceptical, leaving it as the
prerogative of the swarming masses to indulge in
superstitions. Confucius himself declared that it was
man's greatest wisdom to concern himself exclusively
with his human duties and as far as possible to keep
himself out of the way of " spiritual beings."

The disciples of Confucius did not hesitate to
declare that their master made a ternion with Heaven
and Earth. " He may be compared to heaven and
earth, in their supporting and containing, their over-
shadowing and containing, all things. He may be
compared to the four seasons in their alternating
progress and the sun and moon in their successive
shining." Such exaggerated adulation in no way
interferes with an impression of homeliness that is

gradually formed in one's mind of this punctilious prophet who often seems to prophesy backwards. Confucius believed manners to be the very crux of social organization. He believed that men were by nature both benevolent and obedient, and if those in authority could only be persuaded to set them good examples of decorum, the world would be happy. If those in authority were in doubt as to correct behaviour, they had but to look into the past for a hundred perfect patterns.

" If any ruler would submit to me as his director for twelve months, I should accomplish something considerable, and in three years I should attain the realizations of my hopes. . . . It would be no more difficult a thing to bring the Empire into a state of tranquillity than for a man to look upon the palm of his hand." " It is all a matter," he used to say in his ambiguous manner, " of rectifying names." There is good government " when the prince is prince, and the minister is minister; when the father is father, and the son is son."

In his opinion, natural affections, natural dependencies and loyalties, are unfailing warranties for the stability of States :—

> " With the right administration government would be rapid just as vegetation is rapid in its season; yea, the government would display itself like an easily growing rush. . . . The relation between superiors and inferiors is like that between the wind and the grass. The grass must bend when the wind blows across it. . . .

> Great, indeed, was Yacu as a sovereign. . . .
> How glorious were his elegant regulations which
> he instituted. . . . May not Shun be instanced
> ˌas having governed efficiently? What did he
> do? He did nothing but gravely and reverently
> occupy his imperial seat."

The emphasis that Confucius laid upon the value
of the proprieties, met with criticism, even in his
life-time. When it seemed likely that he was going
to be put into a position of power by the Duke Ts'e, a
certain courtier vehemently protested. " Scholars,"
he said, " are impracticable and cannot be imitated.
They are haughty and conceited of their own views.
. . . This Mr. K'ung (Confucius) has a thousand
peculiarities. It would take generations to exhaust
all that he knows about the ceremonies of going up
and going down."

On another occasion, when he was driving about
China looking for a prince who would be willing to
put his theories into practice, his carriage was
stopped by a mad hermit. It was in the district of
Ts'oo, and the man shouted, " O Fung, O Fung,
how is your virtue degenerated! As to the past,
reproof is useless, but the future may be provided
against. Give up, give up your vain pursuit."
Confucius, with the open-mindedness of a true
philosopher, immediately got out of his carriage,
wishing to hear more, but the recluse ran away.

This power of viewing himself objectively was
evidently natural to Confucius. It is noticeable in
the following anecdote. Compelled on a certain

occasion to fly from a victorious army, Confucius
arrived at the city gate in some confusion. His
presence was reported to the Prince in the following
manner : " There is a man standing by the East
Gate, with a forehead like Yaou, a neck like Kaou-
Yaou, and altogether having the disconsolate appearance of a stray dog." When this description of
himself in due course reached the ears of Confucius,
he made this comment : " The bodily appearance is
but a small matter, but to say I was like a stray dog—
capital, capital ! "

Many of his idiosyncratic habits and methods of
thought have been preserved to us by his devoted
disciples. In conversation, we are told, he spoke
" minutely and cautiously." There were four subjects that he would never talk about : " Uncanny
happenings, feats of strength, rebellions, and ghosts."
As a young man he would not shoot at a bird when
it was sitting, or catch a fish in a net, because he
considered such methods gave the creatures no fair
chance of escape. When resting he was careful not
to lie as a corpse lies. On seeing a table well provided with provisions he would turn pale. He
liked his rice ground small and his meat minced and
both dishes served with appropriate sauces. He
insisted upon having ginger always on the table. If
he sat down with a mourner he could never eat to
repletion. In the presence of the blind he would
always stand up.

That he had a weakness for the great ones of the

earth cannot be disputed. It is said that when he
passed the vacant place of the Prince,

> " his countenance appeared to change, and his
> legs bend under him, and his words came like
> those of one who hardly had breath to utter
> them. . . . When he came out from the audience
> and he had descended one step, he began to
> relax his countenance, and had a satisfied look.
> When he had got to the bottom of the steps, he
> advanced rapidly to his place, with his arms
> like wings, and on occupying it, his manner still
> showed respectful uneasiness."

It must also be said, however, that he was quick
to give spiritual and intellectual gifts their due, as is
shown by his quaintly significant remark after his
meeting with the philosopher Lao-tze at Chow:
" To-day I have seen a dragon."

In the analects we are given glimpses of his family
life that are full of interest. After the death of his
mother it was a long time before he would play upon
his lute. He marked the place of her grave with
an enormous barrow that he might never have
difficulty in finding it, a necessary precaution, so he
declared, with a sure premonition of his future,
" to a man who belonged to the North, the South,
the East, and the West." When his first child was
born, the Duke Ch'aou sent him as a gift a carp,
and Confucius immediately named his infant son
Carp.

We should like to hear more about the relationship
between this father and son. A disciple once ques-

tioned the Carp about his father, and the young man
volunteered this story :—

> " He [Confucius] was standing alone once
> when I was passing through the court below
> with hasty steps, and said to me, ' Have you
> read the Odes? ' On my replying, ' Not yet,'
> he added, ' If you do not learn the Odes, you
> will not be fit to converse with. . . . Have you
> read the Rules of Propriety? ' At my replying,
> ' Not yet,' he added, ' Until you have read the
> Rules of Propriety your character cannot be
> established.' "

Perhaps it was in the same courtyard that Yuen
Jang offended Confucius by squatting upon his heels
in his presence. " ' In youth not humble as befits a
junior, in manhood doing nothing worthy of being
handed down, and living on to old age : this is to be
a pest.' With this the Master hit him across the
shank with his staff."

The Carp was reproved for showing inordinate
sorrow at the death of his mother. It has been
suggested that Confucius did not get on very well
with his wife, and when we read his considered judgment upon women and their position we can well
believe this hearsay :—

> " Man is the representation of Heaven, and is
> supreme in all things. . . . Woman yields
> obedience to the instructions of man. . . . On
> his account she is subject to the rule of the three
> obediences. When young, she must obey her
> father and elder brother; when married she

must obey her husband; when her husband is
dead she must obey her son. . . . Women's
business is simply the preparation and supplying
of wine and food."

The Carp died before his celebrated father.

Confucius was no loiterer. He was convinced
that destiny required him to fulfil his particular
mission. "From the man bringing his bundle of
dried flesh in payment for my teaching, I have never
refused my instruction to anyone." At the same time
he insisted upon a certain level of intelligence, and
used to say that after he had showed a pupil one
corner of a subject he considered his obligation ended.
His respect he reserved for those scholars who
pursued wisdom so passionately that they "forgot
old age was coming on."

From his sayings it would be possible for anybody
to formulate a working philosophy of life. They are
as wholesome and easy to digest as pecan nuts falling
out of a Mandarin's silken satchel :—

> All men are good at birth, but not many re-
> main so to the end.

> A knowledge of propriety is the stem of a
> man. Without it he has no means of standing
> firm.

> There being instruction, there will be no
> more distinction of classes.

> As we use a glass to examine the forms of
> things, so must we study antiquity in order to
> understand the present.

Am I a bitter gourd? Am I to be hung up, out of the way of being eaten?

The bird chooses its tree. The tree does not choose the bird.

The superior man is distressed by his want of ability. He is not distressed by man's not knowing him.

What the superior man seeks is in himself. What the mean man seeks is in others.

The way of the superior man is threefold, but I am not equal to it. Virtuous, he is free from anxieties; wise, he is free from perplexities; bold, he is free from fear.

When, on another occasion, somebody asked him, "What do you say concerning the principle that injury should be recompensed with kindness?" he answered with shrewd good sense, "With what, then, will you recompense kindness? Recompense injury with justice, and recompense kindness with kindness." Tsze-Kung once asked him: "Is there one word which may serve as a rule of practice for all one's life?" The Master said: "Is not Reciprocity such a word? What you do not want done to yourself do not do to others."

With regard to those deeper questions beyond the boundaries of the market-day life of the individual or state, Confucius is conspicuously reticent. From the earliest dawn of history, ancestor-worship has been a universal practice in China. Needless to say,

Confucius himself was scrupulous in the fulfilment of such rites. When, however, one of his disciples ventured to ask him for a word of guidance in serving the departed, he was answered with the following evasion : " Until you are able to serve men, how can you expect to serve their spirits ? " When he was asked point-blank whether or not men had knowledge after death, he answered : " You need not wish to know whether the dead have knowledge or not. There is no present urgency about this question. Hereafter you will know it for yourself."

There exists an ancient legend in China that when a sage mounts the throne and right principles are followed throughout the land, a bird like the phœnix, called the Fung Bird, will appear. This bird, so we are assured, was heard singing in the time of King Wân.

Confucius may well have regarded his own life as a failure. The only prince who had given him power had betrayed him for the sake of beautiful women. At the age of fifty, when he " knew the decrees of Heaven," he was raised from being the head magistrate of the city of Chung-tu to being the chief administrator of his native state. His enlightened measures soon made the State of Lu dangerously strong, and a neighbouring marquis devised the cunning plan of sending eighty dancing-girls of easy virtue as a gift to the sage's prince. All State affairs were immediately neglected, and Confucius could do nothing but leave in disgust.

A second tentative patron took the opportunity of consulting Confucius upon military tactics. "I have heard all about sacrificial vessels, but I have not learned military matters." Confucius left the next day. In another state—the State of Wei—the marquis was married to a notorious Chinese Jezebel named Nan-tsze, and it pleased him to have Confucius riding behind himself and his painted lady. Presently the populace began to note this and to chaff the seer, shouting till the pagodas echoed, "Lust in front, virtue behind." Once again Confucius felt constrained to go on his travels.

He lived to the age of seventy-three. The last years of his life were occupied with editing the classical books and with writing the history of his native state. Three times he is said to have worn out the leather thongs that bound together the manuscripts he was studying. About reforming the world he was no longer sanguine. "It is over!" he cried. "I have not seen one who loves virtue as he loves beauty."

One morning Tsze-Kung, his faithful disciple, waked to hear Confucius about early. He got up, and found the sage walking to and fro outside his door, his hands clasped behind his back, and with his mulberry staff dragging after him. The old man was mumbling to himself these words: "The great mountain must crumble, the strong beam must break, and the wise man wither away like a plant." After a little he said, "My time has come to die."

In seven days he was dead. He offered up no prayers. He was sustained by no hope of life after death. At the same time he betrayed no sign of apprehension. Few could have predicted that this neglected old man was to have more influence upon China than all of her Emperors put together.

" Our Master cannot be attained to, just in the same way as the heavens cannot be gone up to by the steps of a stair." When Confucius left his first State employment a sympathetic onlooker remarked to one of his followers, " Heaven intends to use your master as a bell for the people." A few years before, when the Buddha had gone into retirement in the Vindhya Mountains, it had been said that his fame spread " like the sound of a great bell hung in the canopy of the skies." Since that far-off century, how many human ears have listened to the chiming of those two golden bells?

Immediately after his death Confucius was accorded the recognition that had been denied him in his life. The Duke Gae, who had always carefully refrained from consulting him, now lamented : " Heaven has not left to me the aged man. There is none now to assist me on the throne. Woe is me ! Alas ! " He caused a temple to be built over the grave of Confucius and arranged that sacrifices should be offered up to his spirit at each of the four seasons of the year. To this day this worship of " K'ung, the ancient teacher, the perfect sage," is continued by his followers, counted now by the hundred million.

"Great art thou, O perfect Sage! Thy virtue is full; thy doctrine is complete. Among mortal men there has not been thine equal. . . . Full of awe we sound our drums and bells."

G. M. Powys.

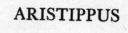

ARISTIPPUS

ARISTIPPUS

" The senses are liars. Do not believe them !""

" Know, then, that all this is but an empty store of words,
which has been drawn up and arraigned against the senses."

So it has gone from the earliest times as though two
opposing " Jacks " were alternately striking the
great, resonant clock-bell of life every few minutes—
ding, dong, ding, dong ! Aristippus, the master of
the Cyrenaic school of hedonistic philosophy, lit
upon his illumination of " the true word " through
his contact with Socrates, and his plain speaking
has had, ever since, a deep effect upon the thought
of mankind. How many Epicureans in every
country have done honour to this teaching from the
sunny seaside colony on the coast of Africa !

Even among Greek philosophers Aristippus was
remarkable for his frolic wit. Less timorous than
Epicurus, he appears in the world of thought as a
kind of Panurge passing gaily from city to city with
a cock's feather in his cap. " He was ever one,"
wrote Diogenes Lærtius, " who derived pleasure
from what is present and did not toil to procure the
enjoyment of something not present."

Apparently it was on the occasion of his visiting

the Olympian games that he first fell under the
influence of Socrates. He had crossed over from
Cyrene to attend the classical celebrations. While
mixing with the fair-field crowd he happened to fall
in with a pupil of the famous philosopher and was
eager in accepting an offer of an introduction to
the notable Athenian. Already acquainted with the
assertion of Protagoras that the sensation of the
moment was "the only ultimate reality," he
required but a hint from his new master to appreciate,
in a flash, how unsure are the foundations supporting
orthodox thought and morality. Socrates had
always insisted that virtue was the true human
good, though conceding happiness to be a subsidiary
end. The daring mind of his new pupil pounced
upon this adjuvant thought, and, forthwith denying
to virtue any especial virtue *in itself*, pronounced
that it was the business of every wise man to direct
his entire attention towards the attainment of
pleasure. Socrates had always placed intellectual
pleasures above those deriving from the body.
Aristippus would have none of this, boldly declaring
that such scholarly pastimes were not comparable
with the direct, and far more satisfying, ecstasies of
the body.

Even the undelusive consummations incident to
higher mathematical studies were depreciated by
him. He placed such "diversions" below handi-
crafts, seeing that in them "the better and the worse
played no part." The practical conduct of life was

all his cry, and its main purpose he took to be a scrupulous garnering of the rich harvest of the senses. In so far as intellectual sophistications interfered with this supreme aim, he rejected them out of hand, holding that any absolute knowledge was beyond man's reach for all time—accepted knowledge being merely a relative convention, an unreliable mental mirage of what appears to each separate individual to be true, feeling offering, in his opinion, the only valid criticism of both behaviour and knowledge. " As modes of being affected alone are knowable," it follows, as the day the night, that the past is nothing, the future nothing, and that the sensual experiences of the moment are alone of consequence. Of such experiences none could possibly rival for depth and intensity the delights of love-making. It appeared to Aristippus that the basic principle of all life was to be found in two states of being, the state of happiness and the state of pain, the one the child of wisdom, and the other the child of folly, the one agreeable and the other repellent to every living thing. Epicurus taught that if the mind could be free from anxiety and the body from physical disorders, happiness would inevitably be present. So tame a form of happiness would have been repudiated with contempt by Aristippus, who believed it was possible to plan for pleasures, and in some cases to snatch them from the hands of envious Fate, as a dog will snatch a cold woodcock from out of a pantry window. It seemed to him that happiness was as accessible to the poor as to the rich and was a condition that could be induced by a cunning wisdom. In order that a man should never become a slave to his passions, complete self-mastery was essential. A man should be able to curb his desires or abandon himself to them in accordance with the dictates of prudence and good sense.

Cyrene, the home of Aristippus, was the most ancient of five Greek colonial towns situated on the coast of Libya. It was built far up on a terraced slope in a locality so virginal fresh that it was calculated to incline men's minds to pleasure-loving conclusions—to those philosophic conclusions, in fact, that Pascal disparaged as being " pernicious to all who have a natural tendency to impiety or vice." The thought of these Cyrenaics became as light as the mountain air they breathed, as light as that wonderful rarefied air that was said to nourish and refine the fleeces of their sheep, fleeces unsurpassed for a particularly high-class staple, and which was also rumoured to impregnate the very mares, as, ready to start at the rustle of a green lizard, they faced the breeze on those upland pasture-grounds with quivering nostrils miraculously receptive to so vital a breath.

As this favoured people rested beneath the shadows of conduit-cooled fig trees, or clambered in holiday mood along steep and lonely slopes far up above the restless waves, they refused to be intimidated by the morbid deceits of either metaphysics or supernatural religions. The human predicament appeared to them clear as day. The gods, if there were gods, remained entirely unimplicated in mortal affairs. Human beings were allotted a few vanishing moments for gladness " in the coasts of light," and then, all their careless surrenders cancelled, were laid away in the sepulchres which, like so many bakers' ovens, honeycombed the sides of their winding mountain roads. How beautiful those familiar rock-strewn slopes were, balanced firm between the blue of the sky and the blue of the Mediterranean, precipitous slopes green with prosperous spurge bushes, whose yellow blossoms to sauntering twilight lovers would appear like the eyes upon the outspread tails of a hundred flaunting peacocks !

What wild imagining was it that could venture to attribute to life any other meaning than that of life ? In such a privileged locality death itself lost half its terror. Gone overnight were the nervous apprehensions inherited from the Stone Ages, apprehensions that had bred in far-off days the superstitious rituals darkening the lives of the ancient inhabitants of the Greek peninsula with rites of sacrificial expiation, rites even yet lingering on in Attica. These legacies of sinister thought-infection melted away in the Cyrenaic sunshine. In an environment where the very corpses in their sandy hollows remained dry and gay it was not easy for spiritual disorders to thrive.

Aristippus brought all considerations down to practical decisions. As Timon of Athens sarcastically remarked, " Such was the delicate nature of Aristippus that he groped after error by touch." And true enough it was that the senses, the senses, the senses were his sole concern. He could never be persuaded to regard with a serious countenance the academic jargon of the schools, but confounded all doubters by boldly cutting the Gordian knot of epistemological speculation with one shrewd stroke. He agreed that the evidence of the senses could not be entirely trusted, the senses at best being irresponsible, though, this admitted, he argued that the sensations of each individual possessed a qualified validity which, combined with other processes of consciousness, afforded the best proof we could ever hope to gain of the existence of the objective world, making up also a sum of knowledge " adequate for all human purposes." " What is perceived is real " —on such a rough-and-ready axiom he set about to construct his philosophic pleasure dome. To seize with a ruthless greed upon every indulgence presented to the senses would clearly be a mistaken method of life, and one calculated to bring down upon the head a thousand distracting complications. The expediency of each action must be judged by the happiness or unhappiness that it is likely to carry in its train. For Aristippus morality was a matter of right judgments, but right judgments uninfluenced by moralic acid or theological decalogues. The first duty of man is to be happy himself, and when this has been achieved every soul who comes in contact with him shares the largesse of his freedom.

A peculiar radiance is given out from a delighted spirit, and this God-like lustre indicates how the demand of the ego may eventually be reconciled to the necessary exactions of society. Aristippus used to teach that it was sufficient " if we enjoy each single pleasure that is presented," and he himself indulged every luxurious whim that came into his head, and yet always studied to retain the play of his inner life uncorrupted. He remained undaunted before each vicissitude of fortune, robes or rags becoming him equally well. There was in his opinion no absolute morality. " The golden rule to remember was that there was no golden rule." Every situation in life was absolutely unique, never to be repeated again through all eternity, and for this reason must be considered entirely on its own merits. Sensitive discriminations would go far to ensure for an individual fortunate days, with a mind at peace and the carnal desires of the body satisfied.

Aristippus himself possessed that " natural superiority " which often accompanies a disregard of conventional prejudices. Cicero, recognizing his personal distinction, coupled him with Socrates, declaring that " the great and divine excellences " of the two men went far to annul their offences " against custom and tradition." " The multitude,"

Heraclitus once said, " are like people heavy with wine led by children knowing not whither they go." Aristippus valued above everything the " subjective reality " of the individual as it gradually took form under the impacts of life. He felt nothing but contempt for the banal conceptions accepted as reality by the world—false conceptions projected by commonplace minds swarming like bees on a June morning.

Aristippus was no insincere or unpractised philosopher. He was able to adapt himself to every occasion. Plato is reported to have said to him : " You alone are endowed with the gift of being at ease in circumstances of wealth as in circumstances of poverty." This faculty of affable adaptation is well illustrated by the anecdotes that have to do with his stay at the court of Dionysius of Syracuse. Though the man " of superior refinement " suffered a thousand humiliations in the proud halls of this tyrant, he preserved intact the essential integrity of his character. Diogenes, jeering from his tub at Aristippus, called him " king's poodle," but at every turn the Cyrenaic's witty quips prove that his mind suffered no degradation. Even when the tyrant spat upon him he merely remarked : " If the fishermen let themselves be drenched with sea-water in order to catch a gudgeon, ought I not to endure to be wetted with negus in order to take a blenny? "; and when Dionysius, exasperated by one of his sallies, sent him to sit at the lowest place at the table, he was overheard saying that the tyrant "must have wished to confer distinction on the last place."

In spite of his free views, he was a man of fastidious personal habits. He felt no compunction about declaring that pleasure was *always good* even if it proceeded from the most unseemly conduct; but certainly his own behaviour was distinguished for its rational self-mastery. In his private life he appears to have been the reverse of riotous. When Dionysius, for once in a genial mood, offered him his choice of three alluring flute-girls, he took them all away with him, excusing himself by saying: " Paris paid dearly for giving the preference to one out of three "; but on reaching the door of his house he let them all go again. In his youth he was privileged to enjoy the favours of Lais, but even in such exceptional circumstances he still remained " a child of herbs and abstinences." This celebrated courtesan used to amuse herself at the expense of those who pretended to have gained a superiority over their passions. " The sages and philosophers," she lightly laughed, " are not above the rest of mankind, for I find them at my door as often as any other Athenians." Aristippus, being reproached by some grudging moralist of the day for his frequent visits to her house, replied after this fashion: " I have Lais, not she me : and it is not abstinence from pleasures that is best, but mastery over them without ever being worsted "; and again when he observed

a young man of his train—a disciple—blushing to
see him enter a bawdy-house, he defended himself
by remarking : " It is not going in that is dangerous,
but the not being able to go out."

It seems he was never at a loss for a pat retort.
When someone criticized him for leaving a room in
the middle of an angry argument, he answered :
" Because it is your privilege to use foul language,
so it is my privilege not to listen." On his first
arrival at the Sicilian palace, Dionysius, wishing to
humiliate him, asked him why he, a philosopher,
should have come to his court. Aristippus answered :
" When I was in need of wisdom I went to Socrates;
now that I am in need of money I come to you."
Dionysius, continuing his banter, asked him to
explain how it came about that philosophers visited
rich men but rich men did not visit philosophers.
" The one," replied Aristippus, " knows what he
needs, while the other does not." And when he was
derided for accompanying a petition with prostra-
tions at the feet of Dionysius he said : " It is not I
who am to blame, but Dionysius, who has his ears in
his feet."

On one occasion when he was sailing to Corinth a
sudden storm arose, and it was observed that he
displayed every sign of extreme perturbation. The
seamen, noticing this, said : " We plain men are not
alarmed; and are you philosophers, then, turned
cowardly ? " To which he coolly replied, in a style
reminiscent of one of Oscar Wilde's effronteries :

" The lives at stake in the two cases are not comparable."

He was reckless and extravagant in his attitude to money, and once when he saw his slave overburdened with a bullion-bag he called to him to " Pour away the greater part of the coin, and carry no more than you can conveniently manage "; and many times he was heard to remark that " Riches were not like shoes which when too large cannot be used." It was observed, however, that in the process of imparting his wisdom to his daughter Arete, he especially taught her " to despise excess." Aristippus died in the eightieth year of his age, 356 B.C. Arete, however, instructed her son with such understanding that he was able to develop still further the philosophic system of his grandfather.

Possibly the most interesting of these later Cyrenaics was Theodorus. Diogenes Lærtius tells us that he wrote a treatise entitled *Of the Gods* which was " not contemptible." Theodorus was a convinced pacifist. He declared himself to be a citizen of the whole world, and thought it reasonable for the good man not to risk his life in the defence of his country, " for he should never throw wisdom away to benefit the unwise."

The exact position of Cyrene was a little to the east of Tripoli, in the vilayet of Barka, and surely the passing of the centuries does not seem to have brought any large increment of wisdom to that quarter of the world. When will men learn that

" every violation of justice strikes at the very life of society itself and threatens the destruction of the indispensable conditions of all happiness "?

Many of the problems of life and death that were approached with so much spirit by these lively thinkers remain still open questions. Men, as of old, are easily betrayed by the more obvious allurements of life. They seek happiness by acquiring more riches than they can possibly use, by exercising power over others, by satisfying uncivilized personal ambitions. Scarce one in a thousand is content with the simple natural heaven-sent rewards of life. The bones of Aristippus have long since crumbled to dust. The airy breath of his wisdom remains with us. Yet how few are the fowlers, either in the Occident or in the Orient, whose nets are fine and strong enough to catch the careless seaside wind of his pure happiness :—

"The world being fleeting, I practise naught but artifice;
I hold only with happiness and sparkling wine;
Forsake not the book, and the lover's lips, and the green
    bank of the field
Ere that the earth enfolds thee in its bosom."

G. M. Powys.

THE BOOK OF ECCLESIASTES

THE BOOK OF ECCLESIASTES

To the pious it has always been a stumbling-block that there should be included in the pages of the Bible such frankly hedonistic precepts as are to be found in the Book of Ecclesiastes. From the first this singular book has been subjected to manipulations at the hands of the orthodox. In many cases the subversive thoughts expressed by the Preacher have been deliberately rendered innocuous by the arbitrary insertion of conventional sentiments. The book as it was originally written was as easy to be understood by the rich as by the poor, by the educated as by the ignorant.

Professor Jastrow accomplished a notable service in sloughing off these misleading passages, thereby enabling us to read the essay as it first stood. Thus treated, the book regains the full force of its strong and simple message. If, as many of us believe, supernatural religions represent the imaginative response of a speculative animal startled out of its slow wits by the endowment of a rudimentary consciousness, then there has been provided us in these venerable pages a philosophic message as simple as the grass and as lucky.

The poetical preacher, with the design of obtaining

a better hearing, utters his wisdom under the shadow
of the " Son of David King in Jerusalem," whose
renown for practical wisdom had considerable
prestige in the East.   From so formidable a vantage
point he felt no compunction about speaking boldly.
All our metaphysical systems and religious faiths,
each contradicting the other, have no more substance
than dreams.   The race of man is truly, as Homer
discerned, in no way superior to the " race of leaves,"
a race fugitive and without signification !   Many of
the great sages have entertained this same conviction.
Others, hesitating to sponsor so desolate a conclusion,
have acquiesced in the more vaulting claims of the
tribe.   In every generation there are found men and
women who derive spiritual refreshment from un-
compromising words spoken without fear.   Impatient
of idealistic conceptions more easy to be believed than
to be proved, they recover a lost sense of dignity
from accepting life upon its lowest terms, making no
more demands for transcendental intervention than
does the water-rat in its aquatic domicile on the
willow-herb bank of a river.   Such undebauched
creatures do not consider matters outside the range
of their common senses :—

" They do not lie awake in the dark and weep for their sins,
  They do not make me sick discussing their duty to God,
  .   .   .   .
  Not one is respectable or unhappy over the whole earth."

There is no good reason why we should not emulate
this sublime detachment from the inactual, a detach-

ment in our case recognizing that knowledge of the Absolute is beyond man's reach. " Far off is that which exists and very deep—who can find it out ? "

The author of Ecclesiastes believes that man holds no privileged place. The atomic " torrents of spring " are in no intelligent way implicated in his saucy destiny, a destiny for which no moral provision has ever been made. There is no survival of the soul after death, nor has man any pre-eminence over the beast. Such a denial is distasteful to those who have become practised in the acceptance of agreeable creeds. Even the writer of Ecclesiastes, too much influenced by the prattling of priests, does not allow his thought to sink to the lowly level where the springs of living water are to be found.

The book opens with a magnificent passage expressing the melancholy that takes possession of sensitive minds when contemplating the recurring transmutations of indestructible matter. " The sun also ariseth, and the sun goeth down, and hasteth to the place where he arose . . . All the rivers run into the sea, yet the sea is not full. . . . All things are full of labour; man cannot utter it. . . . What profit hath a man of all his labour which he taketh under the sun ? One generation passeth away, and another generation cometh : but the earth abideth for ever." The poet then considers the futility of trying to acquire wisdom and of accumulating stores of learning. Well has he apprehended that in Nature's prodigality the knowledge of the scholar is

scattered for ever by Death, scattered not a whit less
carelessly than is the folly of the fool. " For there
is no remembrance of the wise more than of the fool
for ever : seeing that which now is in the days to
come shall all be forgotten. And how dieth the wise
man ? As the fool."

Despite all fancies it is evident that we dance each
one of us to his own predestined tune, and it is not
in the power of any man or of any woman to alter
the essential moulding given to them by the hand of
the potter. Our fate is bound to our backs like a
pilgrim's fardel. " To everything there is a season,
and a time to every purpose under the heaven. . . .
A time to plant, and a time to pluck up that which is
planted . . . there is no man that hath power over
the spirit to retain the spirit; neither hath he
power in the day of death." The Preacher sees
also that evil is more active than good and that to
resist evil is to court worldly disaster, and to
struggle against it is like trying to dam back a tidal
river with half a dozen bundles of broken winter
reeds : for in earth cruelty has always, and will
always, hold empire over compassion. " So I
returned, and considered all the oppressions that
are done under the sun : and behold the tears of
such as were oppressed, and they had no comforter ;
and on the side of their oppressors there was power ;
but they had no comforter."

Nor are the rewards from the possessive instincts
any more reliable. Be a life never so long, an

indulgence of the acquisitive impulse inevitably ends in disillusionment. "As he came forth of his mother's womb, naked shall he return to go as he came, and shall take nothing of his labour, which he may carry away in his hand." We have, indeed, but one absolutely necessary copy-book truth to learn about earth-life—*its instability*. We frisk and feed under as stiff a discipline as Easter lambs in a butcher's paddock. There is no appeal. "For man also knoweth not his time : as the fishes that are taken in an evil net, and as the birds that are caught in the snare ; so are the sons of men snared in an evil time, when it falleth suddenly upon them." In one simple sentence does the Preacher settle the gnarled argument between the living and the dead, "A living dog is better than a dead lion. For the living know that they shall die ; but the dead know not anything."

He brings his practical good sense to bear upon our predicament, and concludes that a man can do nothing better than to enjoy to the full every pleasure that life has to offer. For so blithe an application three things are essential—health, work, and love, elementary requirements that must be diligently sought after. Calculations wise in counsel must be brought to bear upon all the problems of our days, and then, when an opportunity occurs and it is harmonious to do so, we should abandon ourselves utterly to the gratifications of our senses, at the same time not allowing ourselves to become the slaves

of our insatiate appetites. Life, he realizes, is very
complex and often requires the reconciliation of
opposites. " It is a tumultuous passage towards
spiritual peace." The moth that falls scorched to
death has no cause to brag. " Be not righteous over
much; neither make thyself over wise : why
shouldest thou destroy thyself ? Be not over much
wicked, neither be thou foolish : why shouldest
thou die before thy time? . . . All things have I
seen in the days of my vanity : there is a just man
that perisheth in his righteousness, and there is a
wicked man that prolongeth his life in his wickedness." We should be eager and alert to satisfy our
desires, thereby increasing the sum tally of the
world's happiness, but we should satisfy them with
intelligence. It is prudent to snatch from life's
well-spread tables as much as can be snatched without vexation or satiety, remembering always that the
simpler our pleasures the more happy are we likely
to be. " Better is an handful with quietness, than
both the hands full with travail and vexation of
spirit. . . . The sleep of a labouring man is sweet,
whether he eat little or much : but the abundance
of the rich will not suffer him to sleep."

As the book gathers towards its end the fervour
of the prophet unites with the inspiration of the poet.
The true word " was in my heart as a burning fire
shut up in my bones, and I was weary with forbear-
ing, and I could not stay." No longer can he suffer
the young to be betrayed by the admonitions of

those who would slyly disparage the life of the
senses. In every age it has been the same. Mag-
nates with top-knots of almond blossom plot how
best to impede the white ankles of Atalanta. Boys
and girls shall be instructed in his Canticle of
Scepticism. " Rejoice, O young man, in thy youth;
and let thy heart cheer thee in the days of thy youth,
and walk in the ways of thine heart, and in the sight
of thine eyes." If once man could be persuaded to
accept what he has without neurotic evasions he
could live with mirth. The plain gifts of life suffice.
They alone offer us a deep and incontestable solace.
Let us leave the Tree of the Knowledge of Good and
Evil and gather like thoughtless children about the
Tree of Life, where it grows in everlasting sunlight
on its high upland lawn. Rid of illusions we shall
learn then to worship as the early-morning starlings,
with speckled polished backs, worship.

" Behold : that which I have seen : it is good and
comely for one to eat and to drink, and to enjoy the
good of all his labour that he taketh under the sun
all the days of his life, which God giveth him : for
it is his portion . . . this is the gift of God." The
fact that all go to one place should be the clue to
our conduct. With jealous eyes we should guard
against every threat to our personal liberty of
thought or action. Our morality should be as wayward as the wind—a matter of individual taste, of
individual pride, of individual understanding. When
once we are rid of our emotional tensions we shall be

in a position to entertain those unpartisan amoral judgments that can redeem each situation. Long, rich, full, and imaginative lives are required, lives that spread and burgeon and bring joy and shelter to all.

In the sonorous periods of the last great chapter of Ecclesiastes may be found the most poetical and honourable sentences in the Bible. It is as though the lot of each man and of each woman born from the womb had found in this dirge its adequate celebration.

" In the days when the keepers of the house shall tremble . . . and the almond tree shall flourish, and the grasshopper shall be a burden, and desire shall fail." It is interesting to learn that the Rabbinical commentators were accustomed to interpret the allusion to the grasshopper as a direct reference to the masculine organ of carnal desire. And truly it is this very " grasshopper " that animates all life. Here is the solid tap-root of our airy transports, and without its vigour even mystical visions would vanish away. This narwhal's horn, with its un-ceasing life-long sea-shell murmurings of the far-off orchards of Cathay, may verily be said to be our ankh, the emblem of all our joy. It is a divining rod that never fails. It is an enchanter's wand that can transmute the dullest dust into shining sun-motes of purest gold. When its spell is upon us we sleep light, live light, and tread on the grass of familiar honeysuckle lanes as though under a glamour. Wherever there is living existence the spirit of Love is present, and wherever Love is present moments of happiness are possible.

" Truly the light is sweet, and a pleasant thing it is for the eyes to behold the sun."

G. M. Powys.

LUCRETIUS

LUCRETIUS

No great poet more nobly represents the mutinous
Promethean theomachy than does Lucretius. For
two thousand years his passionate sincerity has
roused men out of their servile sloth. His
philosophy—so simple, so deep—transvalues values.
It frees men from uneasy fears and makes it possible
for them " to contemplate all things with a mind at
rest." For the human race has not raised itself out
of the earth's heavy clay clear-eyed. From the first
its power of reasoning was rendered infirm by ata-
vistic animal mistrusts, and few of us may be said to
have retained an heroic vision " beneath the gliding
stars."

Poetry is a heightened awareness of existence, an
intensity of conscious emotion, an intensity of conscious thought. The perceptions of Lucretius were
so vibrant that his poem still trembles with life, and
the " lasting loveliness " of his words comes straight
down to us from his living lips.

It is remarkable how few didactic poems are
entirely free from the taint of theological sub-
servience. Of these *De Rerum Natura* was the
first and still remains the greatest. With what a
splendour of indignation this great liberator of the

human race regarded religion, and with what dauntless *virtu* his strong soul entered each gloomy cave
of superstition to overthrow it " from top to bottom."
He is the dauntless champion of the earthborn, and
he does not hesitate to raise his mortal head to
outstare those two mighty intimidators—God and
Death.

In astronomy, in anthropology, in psychology,
and in physics, he hints at, even anticipates, the
conclusions of modern scientific research. The
whole riot of earth existence was perceived by him
under the bright light of poetic inspiration. No
other writer can so stir us into realizing how valiant
it is possible for our souls to be. He brings a
new confidence to our faltering spirits, and, upon
eagle's wings, carries us up towards the life-giving
sun.

" For not only would all reasoning fall away, life
itself too would collapse, unless you chose to trust
the senses." His concern is to rid human beings of
their most enervating weakness—fear. He would
have us no longer look askance at the Heavens.
The Gods who dwell in the " interspaces between the
worlds . . . where falls not hail, or rain, or any snow,
nor ever wind blows loudly," are careless of mankind.
They have nothing to do with what is happening
upon earth. All comes about through the agency of
natural laws. " Nothing is ever begotten of nothing
by divine will. . . . And if you learn this surely, and
cling to it, Nature is seen, free at once, and quit of

her proud rulers, doing all things of her own accord
alone, without control of Gods."

In accordance with the theory of his master
Epicurus, he explains that the ultimate substance
of the physical universe is composed of atoms,
which, obedient to natural laws, by the force of
clash and collision come together in nebulæ, and
finally build up the universe with its suns and
planets. "For all the nature of the first bodies lies
far away from our senses below their purview."
Nature herself then is seen to be the creator. She it
is who, acting by law but without moral purpose,
"brings forth the fragile things into the coasts of
light."

The soul is but a corporeal aggregate of refined
atoms which at death are dissipated for ever, along
with the rougher atoms of the body. Thus men have
nothing to fear from the Gods either in life or after
death. "What once sprung from earth sinks back
into the earth."

But if we are in the grip of the inevitable move-
ments of atomic matter, then all must be deter-
mined, and this in the opinion of Epicurus would be
a worse tyranny than the tyranny of religion. His
theory of the "swerve of the atoms" saves us from
this trap. It is an hypothesis which in our own day
has been revived in a disguised form. The quantum
theory has been of the greatest convenience to pious
men of science on the look-out for mouse-hole God-
cracks in the floor of matter. "By swerving do the

first beginnings make a certain start of movement to break through the decrees of fate so that cause may not follow cause from infinite time."

Surely, for a living organism, annihilation is the most desperate contingency. The very rats in our cellars shrink from it. Lucretius teaches that, once relieved of the fear of punishment hereafter, we should be able to face the inevitable with philosophic calm. "Death, then, is naught to us, nor does it concern us a whit, inasmuch as the nature of the mind is but a mortal possession." Finally, with contemptuous impatience, he rebukes us for our panic misgivings. "Epicurus himself died, who surpassed the race of men in understanding and quenched the light of all, even as the sun rising in the sky quenches the stars. Wilt thou then hesitate and chafe to meet thy doom? thou whose life is well-nigh dead while thou still livest and lookest on the light, who dost waste in sleep the greater part of thy years, and snore when wide awake."

What, then, should be the moral aim of our lives during the years allowed us? Lucretius answers that the true end of life should be personal happiness. Our senses are eager to instruct us how this difficult state is to be won. Physical pain and spiritual conflict disrupt the harmony of soul and body. Such disturbances are to be avoided by setting limits to our desires and fears, and by knowing " what can be done and what cannot." We must minister to the needs and desires of the body, but always within reason, and must preserve the balance of our souls by evading "the gloomy billows of care." When once a fortunate equilibrium has been achieved, then a natural happiness will become habitual to us.

We must protect ourselves against the more dangerous passions, against avarice, against ambition, and against love. We must grasp the essential facts of life, and, understanding what are the "limits of possession," accommodate ourselves as best we may to the human predicament. "It is far better to obey in peace than to long to rule the world with kingly power and to sway kingdoms." By a blessed dispensation what is necessary to sustain life is cheap and easy to procure—bread, cheese, vegetables, water, and "the poor man's plaid." It is the luxuries that are rare and expensive.

Passionate love remains for mortals an ambiguous pleasaunce; even in its most harmonious moments it is our destiny, as we lie enmeshed in this golden net, still to be tortured by unsatisfied yearnings. "But from the face and beauteous bloom of men nothing passes into the body to be enjoyed save delicate images. . . . Even at last when lovers embrace and taste the flower of their years, eagerly they clasp and kiss, and pressing lip on lip, breathe deeply; yet all for naught, since they cannot tear off aught else, nor enter in and pass away, merging the whole body in the other's frame."

When love is unrequited or frustrated, there are

ills that may be detected even with " closed eyes."
She has thrown out some word " and left its sense
in doubt, and it is planted deep in the passionate
heart and becomes alive like a flame." Lucretius
considers nothing more dangerous to happiness than
this kind of love that ravishes a man or woman down
to the very grass. " Nor is he who shuns love
bereft of the fruits of Venus, but rather he chooses
those joys which bring no pain."

The true beauty and power of the poem, however,
do not lie in these cunning reservations, but rather
in his broad survey of life. Though his method is
scientific, it is the imaginative rapture of Lucretius,
his religious awe before the creative energy of Nature,
that gives the work its prophetic power. The whole
of existence is seen by him as a kind of epic ballad.
From the gravitational stir of primal atoms creating
worlds out of the matrix of chaos, to the lowly
beasts of the field leaping quick from the " earth's
wombs," all is impregnated with poetry.

Even in the light of our present-day knowledge
it would be difficult to outline man's early development with more insight than does Lucretius, with
more insight and with more imagination :—

" And during many lustres of the sun rolling
through the sky they prolonged their lives
after the roving manner of wild beasts . . . what
sun and rains had brought to birth, what earth
had created unasked, such gift was enough to
appease their hearts . . . and like bristly boars
these woodland men would lay their limbs

naked on the ground . . . nor could they look
to the common weal, nor had they knowledge
to make mutual use of any customs or laws. . . .
Yet never were many thousands of men led
beneath standards and done to death in a single
day. . . . Then after they got themselves huts
and skins and fire . . . so hatred for their acorns
set in and old couches strewn with grass and
filled with leaves were desolate . . . then first
the race of men began to soften. For fire
brought it about that their chilly limbs could
not now so well bear cold under the roof of
heaven, and Venus lessened their strength, and
children, by their winning ways, easily broke
down the haughty will of their parents. . . .
Lastly thereafter property was invented and
gold found which easily robbed the strong and
beautiful of honour. . . . For the race of men,
worn out with leading a life of violence, lay faint
from its feuds; wherefore the more easily of its
own will it gave in to ordinances and the close
mesh of laws. . . . Next, what cause spread
abroad the divine powers of the Gods among
great nations, and filled cities with altars, and
taught men to understand sacred rites at yearly
festivals, rites which are honoured to-day in
great empires and at great places; whence even
now there is implanted in mortals a shuddering
dread, which raises new shrines of gods over all
the world, and constrains men to throng them
on holy days; of all this it is not heard to give
account in words."

He calls to men to abjure cowardice and lifting
up their heads, to accept their free inheritance with
unvanquished hearts, like gods.

G. M. Powys.

LUCIAN

LUCIAN

In these days when philosophic opinions sharply conflict, and some declare that we live in a universe subject to scientific research, while others assert that the physical world testifies to the truth of our supernatural creeds, we may well derive profit from re-reading the works of Lucian. In the second century of our era the religious conclusions of the civilized world were just as uncertain as are our own. Few educated people believed in the existence of the old pagan gods. Christianity had not yet had time to show the power of its appeal. The moral exhortations of the wisest teachers were seldom to be reconciled with their personal conduct, and false prophets, like the notorious Alexander, were as ready as those of to-day to batten upon the ignorance and credulity of the populace.

Lucian was born at Samosata in the province of Babylon in A.D. 125. As a young man he travelled to Egypt and other centres of religious life. He was for a period in Rome, and afterwards spent ten years as a lecturer in Gaul. In his later life he resided in Athens, a favoured man of letters, eventually being rewarded by the Emperor Severus with a sinecure appointment as secretary to the Prefect of Egypt. His works—and he was a generous author—are written in pure Attic Greek. The Christians circulated a legend that in his old age he was devoured by dogs, but, although the date and manner of his death are unknown, we have no reason to believe this piece of malicious tittle-tattle.

Lucian's mind was essentially civilized. He was interested in every aspect of human life, examining all that came to his attention with an alert and tolerant intelligence.

His life was separated from the life of Jesus by approximately the same number of years as ours is from the life, let us say, of Lord Byron, and when this fact is appreciated, the casual references to Christianity that this scoffer makes have a singular interest. For example, what a shock of contemporaneous authenticity purged of cant comes to us when, in speaking of the Christians, he refers to Jesus as their " crucified sophist "; and again, there is something deeply moving in his application of the epithet " great " to Christ when we recollect that it is from the mouth of a man of the world whose unemotional disposition was incapable of understanding either poetry or passion. " You know they [the Christians] still reverence that great man, him who was crucified in Palestine for introducing these new doctrines into the world."

His relationship with Proteus, the Christian apostate, must have given him an opportunity for investigating the subtleties of this new creed. He travelled back to Athens with this strange man, notable for burning himself alive. On their arrival in the city Peregrinus Proteus had it publicly announced that he intended to practise the rite of self-cremation. He then had an enormous pyre prepared in front of the Hippodrome, and after the games were over walked boldly towards it wearing the dress of a cynic. His friends did what they could to dissuade him from his purpose, but his enemies kept urging him to keep his promise. Sprinkling the brushwood with frankincense, he deliberately entered the flames, uttering as he did so certain words of mystical implication.

A scene of this kind was exactly calculated to exasperate Lucian, and after the spectacular performance was over he walked back to the city spreading a report that he himself had seen a vulture leave the fire and fly towards the sun. This playful invention, he noted, was soon circulating as an authenticated fact. Lucian found it difficult to account for his friend's extraordinary conduct. Eventually, after his cynical manner, he attributed it to a love of notoriety, a judgment hardly in accord with the mystical passion of the man's last words.

To an intellect dominated by logic, emotional feeling or emotional action must have its origin either in insincerity or in insanity. It was, indeed, incidents of this kind that confirmed Lucian's conviction as to the irremediable folly of the human

H

race.   Wherever he went he saw people acting in a
manner that seemed to him little short of imbecile.
In Egypt he observed them worshipping cats, mon-
keys, water-jugs, and was amazed beyond all measure
by the outcry and wailing that went up over the
death of Apis, the common town bull !

Lucian, in fact, had reached that enviable
philosophic state which enables a man to survey
the human scene with unimplicated detachment.
Profoundly disillusioned, he considered human life
of too short duration for anybody to hope to understand its deeper secrets, and consequently he advised
men to cultivate their gardens and fulfil as best
they might the simple duties of citizenship.

Nothing diverted him more than to elaborate
upon any scrap of legendary hearsay that seemed
to render the gods ludicrous.   He especially relished
comic stories about them, and was never tired of
referring to the trick Prometheus played upon the
President of the Immortals when at table he served
him with the worst pieces of the joint, pieces little
better than bare bones and gristle, covered up in
" shining fat."   The floor of heaven he describes as
adjusted with round apertures fitted with lids,
" like the coverings of wells."   At certain set times
Jupiter listens to the human prayers that come
floating up through these apertures, comfortably
settling himself upon each golden throne, placed by
the side of the holes for his convenience.   He hears
" One sailor praying for a north wind, another for a

south wind : the farmer for rain, and the fuller for
sunshine."

For all his worldliness, Lucian had a moral
austerity. This is clearly revealed in his description
of the miseries and humiliations attendant upon the
life of a sycophant, upon the lives of upper servants,
companions, and tutors, people who, for the sake of
a soft livelihood, must of necessity suffer the most
galling personal indignities. " I had rather," he
cries, " for my part, have an onion and some salt,
and be allowed to cut it when and how I please. . . .
Is there no pulse still growing, no wholesome herbs
on which a man may sustain life, no streams of pure
water left, that you should be driven to this direst
strait for existence? "

He is of opinion that the majority of men are
doomed to live upon trust, that the gods want prayers
and not philosophy, and that in reality everything
goes with wind and tide and " as chance may waft
it." He is at pains to warn men against too confident a dependence upon sexual gratifications, upon
that " tree of perpetual thirst, whose flowers are
many strange desires." Speaking as one who pos-
sesses the tranquil mind of a philosopher, he boldly
reminds us that it is not everybody " who is mad-
dened by the sound of the Phrygian flute." In truth
he girds at those who are, as being for the most part
" very bunglers in sensuality, who know not the laws,
and confound her ordinances, flinging down their
souls to be trampled beneath the heels of luxury."

All life to Lucian was a pageant of folly, a kind of Shrove Tuesday pancake carnival, each man, each woman, an inconsequent puppet held up by a transparent little cobweb from Fate's spindle, and zealous to ruin their hazardous unreturning moments by desires, by ambitions, and by lust for gold—" an object of sallow complexion, and of a burdensome weight." He meets an official preening himself in his smart uniform and, taking him by the sleeve, gravely reminds him that his attire " did not make its original wearer anything but a sheep." He is convinced that Jupiter's preoccupation with mankind does not extend so far as " to sift the good from the bad," and that his worshippers go about over the face of the earth, their ears bunged up with that most superlative wax, the substance of which is ignorance and deceit. He is never tired of admonishing his readers to live with understanding—to live, that is to say, with the knowledge of death before their eyes. " A very short survey of life has convinced me of the absurdity, and meanness and insecurity, that pervades all human objects such as wealth, office, power. . . . If only men would start with a clear understanding that they are mortal, that after a brief sojourn on the earth they will wake from the dream of life, and leave all behind them—they would live more sensibly, and not mind dying so much."

Yet the description he gives us of the other world is hardly encouraging. He envisages it as a place

of monotony where there is neither strength nor
beauty, where one is no better than another, " all
under the same gloom." He can make us laugh by
his tale of the dead tyrant's escape and how he
almost got back to earth, but it is not reassuring to
learn that a couch in a girl's bower can be summoned
to give evidence at the final judgment seat !

We see them, these troops of the departed, with
their " strengthless heads," being hustled along like
so many goats, and when, with Lucian, we have
made ourselves merry at their expense, we find that
the wisest of all these dead men's utterances is upon
the lips of an aged fisherman. Here we come upon
words of simple truth, an answer to man and an
answer to God, natural and not to be gainsaid.
Diogenes notices him amongst the shades, and is
surprised to observe that although apparently the
oldest of them all, he yet wears a dolorous countenance. The dialogue is as follows :—

> *Diogenes :* I must interrogate this most
> reverend senior of them all—Sir, why weep,
> seeing you have died full of years? . . . I see
> you were wealthy, and do not like leaving
> your boundless luxury to die.
> *Pauper :* You are quite mistaken, I was near
> ninety, made a miserable livelihood out of my
> line and rod, was excessively poor, childless, a
> cripple, and had nearly lost my sight.
> *Diogenes :* And you still wished to live?
> *Pauper :* Aye; sweet is the light and dread
> is death; would that one might escape it.

G. M. Powys.

JULIAN THE APOSTATE

JULIAN THE APOSTATE

JULIAN the Apostate has always been a baffling figure to historians, both Christian and secular, a paradoxical figure, noble and ignoble, rational and irrational. He was what we would now describe as " a character "—a cow with a crumpled horn, a lion disguised as an ass. In some ways he was singularly unfitted for the task he undertook—the task of withstanding that baleful " epidemic of unreason " which in due course became responsible for the Dark Ages.

Julian throughout his life may be said to have remained " a spoilt priest," no amount of oblations by means of the *taurbolium* being found sufficient to wash the lustral waters of Christian baptism from his brow or the aroma of the sacramental Christian wine from his golden goat's beard. He was possessed by a sense of mysticism akin to what Christians profess to feel. Nobody could have been farther from the classical state of innocent life-acceptance. He was grossly superstitious, and, despite his adoration of King Helios, ill at ease in the sun's solid domain of earth-reality. He was attracted to all those mock forms of spiritualism that throughout the centuries have given consolation to men. It was this same

infirmity of mind that prompted him to rejoice
at the destruction of the works of Epicurus, and that
rendered his excitable strivings against the neurosis
which had already obtained so insidious a hold over
the senile Roman Empire not altogether satisfactory.

I was once talking to my brother John, who
has always thought it safe for us to put our faith in
the supernatural. I remarked that I could never,
in any circumstances, believe in God, seeing that
so many horrible cruelties took place about me every
hour of the day. To my surprise, he responded to
my words with a show of genuine enthusiasm,
revealing, however, by what he said the indurated
theurgic temper of his mind. " I feel," he exclaimed, " exactly as you do, but it is not the
slightest use declaring yourself to be an Atheist. If
you really wish to annoy God, you must be a
Polytheist. God's prevailing emotion has always
been jealousy, and the mere whisper of the suspicion
that there might exist other deities than himself
throws him into a towering passion." If we should
subscribe to this view, Julian must most certainly
have exasperated the Almighty; for, although he
confined his personal applause to Apollo, Hermes,
and Pallas Athene, he would not willingly have had
the altars of any semi-demi pagan deity neglected.
Indeed, so energetic was he in offering bloody
sacrifices that he earned for himself the nickname of
" The Slaughterer," and upon his setting out for
Persia, the young men did not hesitate to buzz after

him this quip : " The white cattle to Cæsar, greeting.
If you conquer there is an end of us."

Just as certain human beings shiver at the sight
of cats, so there have always been those who cannot
abide Christians.

> " The only man that I ever knew
> Who did not make me almost spew
> Was Fuseli : he was both Turk and Jew.
> And so, dear Christian friends, How do you do ? "

Julian's antipathy was empiric and congenital. The
Christ party had murdered his father and his eldest
brother; but, apart from any resentment on this
score, he felt the utmost contempt for a religion
which divided its worship between an anthropo-
morphic deity, " arbitrary and capricious," and a
dead Jew.

The more he had to do with the Christians the
more obnoxious they became to him, with their
unseemly rivalries and endless doctrinal wrangles.
" Hear me," he cried at one of the synods when his
rational arguments were well-nigh drowned by their
high-pitched, angry voices. " The Franks heard
me, the Allemanni heard me ! " Their morbid
preoccupation with churchyard bones was especially
distasteful to him. With a considerable show of
reason, the philosophic Emperor declared this
peculiar predilection to be in no way justified by the
evidence of the New Testament. " Let the dead
bury their dead " had been the words of Jesus, and

whitewashed sepulchres in the valley of Jehoshophat
were used by him as symbols of corruption. The
Christians, Julian affirmed, were disposed to reject
all Jewish ritual that interfered with the appetites.
" They took to themselves the licence to eat what
they wished, and never feared defilement." They
combined, so he asserted, " Jewish sauciness " with
an unpleasant kind of prurient purity.

Julian's attitude to the Jews was an odd one. It is
supposed he favoured their fads in order to spite the
Christians ! Probably he encouraged the abortive
attempt to rebuild Solomon's Temple for some such
reason, but this in no way meant that he was averse
to exercising his wit upon the " indistinct ravings "
to be found in their sacred books. He clearly noted
every eccentricity of their Jehovah, pointing out that
his idea of government was an emotional rather than
a rational one—a matter of rewards and reprisals
rather than of impartial judgments. Also, in sharp
contrast with what might have been anticipated from
the first civilized resident of Paris, Julian pertly
inquired how it came about that God should form a
woman as a helpmate to man, knowing well that she
would be the cause of Adam's fall, and that her sex
from age to age would be little else than a flickering
torment to the sons of men. He could not believe
that any large-hearted, generous deity would be content to squander " all his favours on one little race
in one little corner of the world to the neglect of the
rest of mankind." The Decalogue he dubs as un-

original, and comments on the folly of the Tower of
Babel story, asserting that all the clay of the world
would not supply enough bricks to reach up to the
lowest horn of the crescent moon. He despised the
New Testament for quite other reasons. He did not
attack the miracles of Jesus for being unreliable
fabrications of a crafty and ambitious priesthood,
but rather as being themselves mean and paltry
prodigies.

There is an essential simplicity in Julian's nature
that is pleasing. The devotion he felt for his
mother, the Lady Basilina, "withdrawn in the
bloom of youth by the motherless maiden Goddess,"
is touching, and so is his affection for his hereditary
country home in Bithynia, grown over with "bind-
weed, thyme, meadow grass, and orchards," and
rendered cool by innumerable fresh springs of water.
His loyalty to his dissolute half-brother Gallus is
remarkable when we consider how natural it would
have been for boys of such different tastes, shut up
together in a lonely Cappadocian Castle, to quarrel.
"The Gods preserved him from being corrupted by
leading him to philosophy," wrote one historian.

When eventually, at the age of twenty-five, he was
summoned by his cousin Constantius to share with
him the imperial purple, how characteristic it was
that he should have been overheard invoking the
name of Plato when trying to learn a wearisome
military drill. Truly he was a strange mixture—
a pseudo man-of-letters, a pseudo metaphysician, a

pseudo soldier who would regularly burn the midnight
oil over his literary essays no matter how hazardous
the campaign. He was dominated by two authentic
passions—an overwhelming admiration for the
classical past and an overwhelming desire for fame.
It was the strength of the latter emotion that explains, if it does not justify, the less worthy episodes
of his life—such, for instance, as his composition of
insincere orations to Eusebia and Constantius, as
well as the alacrity with which he accommodated
himself to the exactions of the Imperial position.
Julian's values, however, would never have been
found but on a high plane, " the last infirmity of a
noble mind," whereas his philosophic monitors, such
as Maximus of Ephesus, at the first jump of his
success wished plain living to the devil and came
scrambling through the buttery hatch of his young
master's palace. The Emperor's stern asceticism is a
matter for astonishment, and it is apparently impossible for him to be budged from the narrow path
of personal abstinence. As Gibbon remarked, no
frightened and tender-eyed female captive was
ever conducted to his tent. Nor was he less exacting
over the pleasures of the table. While in the north,
he refused to receive pheasants into his larder on the
ground of their being a meat too hot and luxurious,
while in his last campaign under a burning desert
sun he was content to subsist on a little " thin
broth."

Small wonder that the voluptuous inhabitants of

Antioch, given over to every kind of indulgence, disliked him; and how in keeping it was with the spirit of Julian to answer their impertinences with a literary essay packed close with humorous sallies against himself. The supercilious manners and fanciful foibles favoured by high society never appealed to the philosophic Emperor, and an ungainliness in his personal deportment would not in any case have allowed him to compete with those people whose accomplishments he despised. He was at home in the dim caves of Mithras or by the high altar of some Greek deity. He felt at ease with the rude, rough rank-and-file of his soldiery, but disliked his ornamental body-guard sent to him by Constantius—" men good for little else but praying." It is significant that he selected for his Imperial Crown a severe " military collar."

He is said to have declared that he never regretted any act of generosity. In his administration he was consistently tolerant. Christians dolefully complained that he studied to deprive them " of the glory of Martyrdom." It is true that when George, the rascally Archbishop of Alexandria, was lynched by the pagan mob, who in a mood of brutal and contemptuous ribaldry bound his corpse to a camel's arse, Julian rebuked the rioters with words only, excusing their excesses on the score of provocation.

This George of Cappadocia had raised himself to his exalted position by cringing and craft, and it was

I

only after his death that he " assumed the mask of a
martyr, a saint, and a Christian hero," so that the
far-famed titular saint of England was in actual
origin nothing better than a dishonourable bacon
contractor. Julian's general attitude to the
Christians, " that miserable parcel of fanatics," is
clearly revealed in the following instructions sent
out to the governors of the provinces : " In the name
of the Gods, I do not desire the Galileans to be killed
or beaten contrary to justice, or that they suffer any
other evil, but I emphatically assert that God-fearing
persons are to receive greater honour; for it is
through the Galilean folly that all things have been
well-nigh overturned." To which St. Athanasius
retorted with a confidence, alas, only too well
justified : " Let us retire. It is but a small cloud
that will soon pass away." Julian once expressed a
wish " that all the new doctrines were embodied in
Athanasius, so that they might be crushed at one
blow." Too clearly he saw the crepuscular fog of
superstition that would gather over Europe if the
machinations of the Galileans were successful. He
urged the Alexandrians to keep clear heads and to
reject Christianity out of hand, reminding them of
" the ancient lordship over Israel."

The Christian bishops had acquired free passes for
travelling along his great Imperial trunk roads.
These privileges Julian cancelled, and he also forbade
Christians to teach the classics in the schools,
suggesting that it would be more seemly for them to

concentrate their attention upon their own out-
standing works—the Gospels of St. Matthew and
St. Luke! Gibbon says of Julian : " His pity was
degraded by contempt; his contempt was embittered
by hatred." He surely could not abide Christian
fooling in any of its manifold forms It was as
unpleasing to him as beer, which he regarded as a
heady beverage not to be compared with the pure
wines of Dionysos. Possibly the edict most resented
by the Christians was his insistence upon their
adopting the name of Galileans in all official dealings.
To a sect that aspired to become a universal religion,
this title, with its provincial connotation, was
humiliating; for, as Mr. Martin, the former devout
believer of Oriel College, Oxford, is eager to remind
us in his book, a summary of the Christian prospects
can be found " in a simple historic statement—the
Creed."

Certainly there is an incorrigible mental in-
fantilism about the thinking of Julian's pious
opponents unto this day. They have even attempted
to discredit the notable words of this " last of the
Romans " as, at the early age of thirty-two, he lay
dying by the strong-flowing River Tigris : " I die
without remorse, as I lived without guilt. . . .
Detesting the corrupt and destructive maxims of
despotism, I have considered the happiness of the
people as the end of government. . . . I now offer
my tribute of gratitude to the Eternal Being, who
has not suffered me to perish by the cruelty of a

tyrant, by the secret dagger of conspiracy, or by the slow tortures of lingering disease. He has given me, in the midst of an honourable career, a splendid and glorious departure from this world; and I hold it equally absurd, equally base, to solicit or to decline the stroke of fate." These inspiring words of the " Good King and mighty warrior " won from the lips of the most enlightened Christian of our times the following disparaging observation : " In the insensibility of conscience, in their ignorance of the very idea of sin . . . we recognize the mere philosopher." That one + one equals guilt has ever been typical of the Christian mind. Indeed, it is from such spiritual disorders that the nervous religion draws its nourishment, just as exotic toadstools in an overshadowed wood draw their prosperity from pieces of buried timber lying in an obscure state of corruption *under ground*. What Heraclitus said years ago of the followers of the mystery religions of his time is not inapplicable to our own tribes of mischievous pretenders : " When defiled they purify themselves with blood, just as if one who had stepped in mud were to wash himself in mud." These frenzied idolaters have always practised magical rites of a kind far too sophisticated ever to have been acceptable to the imagination of the heroic poet whom they so fondly claim to have been the Son of God.

G. M. Powys.

OMAR KHAYYAM

OMAR KHAYYÁM

WHEN I was journeying to Palestine I visited the ruins of Pompeiopolis. This city, which is situated in Asia Minor, not so very far from Anthony and Cleopatra's romantic stream, was destroyed by Tigranes in the year 56 B.C. It stands to-day desolate, its huge classical columns lying where they fell two thousand years ago, its streets overgrown with flowering myrtle, and the avenue of its amphitheatre yellow with fleabane. As I made my way through the ruins, so blandly resigned in the sunshine, a heron rose suddenly into the sky. She had been fishing from the lowest step of a flight of stone stairs against which the waters of the Mediterranean, blue even to the drops falling from a splashing oar, were gently lapping. Although so far from Persia the most inspired tetrastich of Fitzgerald's "Rubáiyát" immediately came into my head.

> " They say the Lion and the Lizard keep
> The Courts where Jamshÿd gloried and drank deep :
> And Bahram, that great Hunter—the Wild Ass
> Stamps o'er his Head, but cannot break his Sleep."

In oriental countries that transmutation of matter,

to which all upon the earth is subject, seems to be
presented more dramatically than in the better-
organized countries to which we are accustomed.
" All things flow away, nothing remains." We
give lip service to words of this kind, and yet most of
us require such startling object lessons as are everywhere provided in the East, where the litter of the
centuries remains permanently conspicuous, before
ever we can get this view of life firmly lodged in our
heads.

Nishapour, the ancient natal town of Omar
Khayyám, is the very spot for such instruction.
Nishapour means " City of the Aryans," a fact
indicating that it was one of the first settlements of
the invading prehistoric Lords from the Steppes.
The celebrated astronomer knew Nishapour in its
glory, and throughout his life it remained a city of
pride, the " most myghty carbuncle " of the Province
of Khorasan. At the beginning of the thirteenth
century Ghengiz Khan and his Tartar soldiery took
it and sacked it in so terrible a manner that, in spite
of its strategic position on the caravan route between
Persia and India, it never recovered its early importance. To-day it is a comparatively insignificant
eastern township built of unburnt bricks and
surrounded by a vast acreage of ruins out of the
past.

Omar Khayyám lived during the decades of the
conquest of England by the Normans. Nishapour
was then in the heyday of its prosperity, its popula-

tion at the lowest computation numbering one
hundred thousand souls.

It was here that, contenting himself with a
pension of one thousand two hundred mithicals of
gold a year, a sum approximating to six hundred
pounds sterling with us, he lived at ease under
the protection of his generous patron; and even
when his wise friend, the celebrated statesman,
Massan Tousi, as an old man fell a victim to the
knife of the first of the " assassins," he still
managed until his death in 1123 to avoid personal
molestation.

Scholars are of the opinion that he composed his
celebrated poem at intervals throughout his life, a
rubáiyát or quatrain being regarded in Persian
literature as a completed isolated unit, as it were a
single jewel, a turquoise let us say, from the mines on
the hillside above Nishapour to be polished and
repolished, for its own signal beauty, before being
strung with others into a necklace of great price.
Omar Khayyám is reputed to have been an eager
student of the Greek classics, and, as was the case
with the author of Ecclesiastes a thousand years
earlier, seems to have given especial attention to
the more wayward Greek thinkers. " How long,
how long, the Philosophy of the Greeks? Study
also the Philosophy of the true Faith ! " one of his
devouter contemporaries is said to have cried out
to him.   There exists other evidence to show that
he was regarded with suspicion by the stricter

Mohammedans! Indeed, one doctor of the Koran
does not hesitate to call him " an unhappy philosopher, atheist, and materialist " !

Omar Khayyám is believed at one time to have
made a journey to Mecca, and to have returned—so
at least is suggested by Mr. John Payne, a rather
contentious critic of the last century—with more
sympathy for the Vedantic learning than for the
fables of Islam, substituting the Hindoo metaphysic
and their notion of universal oneness for the cat and
dog, good and evil simplicities of the easier faith.
Perhaps his contact with the philosophic casuistry
of India may explain the pessimistic trend detracting
from the power of his famous poem. The mood of
Omar Khayyám is always far from that of blithe
Dionysos. He celebrates Love and Wine as a man
who despairs of finding a more elevated meaning to
life. It is in truth with unmistakable reluctance
that he rejects the intellect " haunting the path of
happiness." In a flash it had been suddenly
revealed to him that human transcendental speculation was unreliable from top to bottom.

> " Why, all the Saints and Sages who discuss'd
> Of the Two Worlds so learnedly, are thrust
> Like foolish Prophets forth; their Words to Scorn
> Are scatter'd, and their Mouths are stopt with Dust."

The old mathematician may have been able to
write a learned treatise on algebra, and present with
propriety the new calendar of Jeláleddin which, as

Gibbon affirms, "surpasses the Julian and approaches
the accuracy of the Gregorian style," but for all this
his mind was not firm enough to sustain the decline
and fall of cherished human illusions. To view
theological dogmas as "agreed upon fables," and yet
to praise life without reservations was beyond his
pluck. Many of his verses reveal his bitter repudia-
tion of the terms upon which all animal creation
accepts and welcomes life.

> " What, without asking, hither hurried *Whence*?
> And, without asking *Whither* hurried hence!
> Oh! many a Cup of his forbidden Wine
> Must drown the memory of that insolence!"

How was it that this indulged philosopher demanded so much?   His lot was a fortunate one.   He
was too wise to be taken in by the ordinary baits
which ruin the lives of most human beings, baits
which catch men and women as neatly as roach are
hooked with balls of dough mixed with cotton wool!
He was not avaricious, he was not ambitious.   He
owned sufficient practical sagacity to constrain him;
" for prudential motives," to bridle his tongue, so
that he was in little danger of having it pulled out
from the back of his heretical head, as was done to
the jesting victim of Jamá lu'l-Mulk who had been
rash enough to let fly a quip at the respected
Nidhan-ùl-Mulk!   He had a mind free from moral
inhibitions, while he was gifted with the awareness
of the passing moment that admitted him to the

heightened experiences belonging to the life of a poet.
And yet even so he was not satisfied to take the cash
and let the credit go, as he bragged. See what
enviable days the rogue lived snug as a maggot in an
apple, under the benevolent eye of a Vizier of the
widest culture, the founder of colleges in Baghdad,
the author of the classic, *Treatise and Art of Government*, and, so it is reported, the inventor of the
present Persian method of keeping accounts ! And
what luck to have been alive in the reigns of the two
best Seljúq Sultans ! He first had for a sovereign
Alp Arslán, a great bestower of pensions at the
Feast of Ramadán, a man of remarkable stature tall
as a date-palm, and with moustaches so long " that
he was compelled to tie up their ends when he wished
to shoot " : he was the great warrior who, with fifteen
thousand men, defeated the Byzantine Emperor with
his army of two hundred thousand picked soldiers,
only to meet his ill-fated accidental death on
Christmas Day 1072.

" Thou hast seen Alp Arslán's head in pride exalted to the
   sky;
   Come to Merv, and see how lowly in the dust that head
   doth lie."

His son Maliksháh, who succeeded him, might equally
well have been called " conquering lion," though he
was distinguished still more for his enlightened rule,
as is shown by his establishment of Omar Khayyám's
observatory, and by the fact that he had wells dug
along the highways used by pilgrims. He, like his

father, prided himself on his archery, delighting in
the chase, and yet he was sensitive enough to feel
uneasy in his conscience about his wholesale blood-
sports, saying on one occasion, " I fear God Almighty,
for what right had I to destroy the lives of these
animals without necessity or need of them for
food? "   Cherished by such great rulers, had Omar
any good cause or justification for complaint?

> " Oh, Thou, who Man of baser Earth didst make,
>   And ev'n with Paradise devise the Snake :
> For all the Sin wherewith the Face of Man
>   Is blacken'd—Man's forgiveness give—and take ! "

His native city enjoys a climate almost un-
matched in Persia; in the time of Omar, Nishapour,
occupying a space four miles square, was in very
truth a garden city!   The streets in the long soft
twilights, and under the large honey-coloured
Asiatic moons, smelt of the scents of roses; the
oriental breezes lightly lifting the fragrant burdens
of a thousand closed-in gardens where every portico
contained a lover " resting in his sweetheart's
arms," and all night long the splashing from the
cisterns continued the monotonous murmuring
sound of water falling upon stone.

The poets of Persia are never tired of praising
Nishapour.   One of them named Katibi describes
himself as coming " like attar, from the Rose-land
of Nishapour "; and declares, " If Paradise is to be
found on the face of the earth, it is in Nishapour;
if not there, it exists not."   Even to-day, nourished

by small rains, the neighbourhood of the town for
a wide circuit is thick-grown with lemon and orange
orchards.   It is said that a traveller may ride out of
the city along the beautiful valley of Meshad and
always be in the shade.   The mountains, because of
their extreme fertility, are green, cultivated to their
very summits.   Date palms, almond trees, and fig
trees grow everywhere, and from the tops of the
walls melons hang burgeoning in the sun.   Anyone
up betimes is rewarded by an inconceivable fresh-
ness.   The streets of the bazaars give out the odour of
the stamped and perfumed saddlery so highly prized
by mediæval horsemen ; while in the fields lilies of
the valley grow thick as garlic, and the chattering
calls from the sand-grouse rise from the dew.   Omar
Khayyám knew well such lovely places of freedom,
knew, none better, the same sensation of spiritual
release that comes to us in England when, after suffering some irksome social discipline, we escape to the
open highway, seeking refuge on a waste patch like
any tramp who invites his soul with crooked knee,
at liberty and couched in dust and camomile.

> " Well, let it take them ! What have we to do
> With Kaikobád the great, or Kaikhosrú ?
> Let Zál and Rustum bluster as they will,
> Or Hatim call to supper—heed not you.
>
> With me along the strip of Herbage strown
> That just divides the desert from the sown,
> Where name of Slave and Sultan is forgot
> And Peace to Mahmúd on his golden Throne ! "

There is a story of an interview between Tamerlane and the poet Hafiz. On entering the city Shiraz, Tamerlane summoned the poet. The Conqueror came fresh from his favourite pastime of building pyramids of skulls, on this occasion a pyramid made up of seventy thousand skulls belonging to the human beings whom he had slaughtered in revenge for the deaths of a few dozen of his testy Tartars ! To the poet he quoted the poet's own lines

" If that unkindly Shiraz Turk would take my heart within
     her hand,
   I'd give Bukhárá for the mole upon her cheek or
     Samarquand ! "

He asked him brusquely what he meant by esti-mating the value of these cities so cheap when he, Tamerlane, had laboured and sweated to subdue them. Hafiz, intimidated, bowed low before the grim soldier, saying, " Alas ! O Prince, it is this prodigality which is the cause of the misery in which you now see me." Placated utterly by this indirect testimonial to his own get-and-kill, kill-and-get manner of life, Tamerlane gave orders that Hafiz should be treated with every consideration. The anecdote illustrates to perfection the struggle that is forever proceeding between the advocates of action and the advocates of pleasure.

" The drum ever cries, but what good doth it do,
     Since its carcase is hollow and empty within ?
     If wisdom be thine, then the Real pursue,
     And be not deceived by a flatulent skin."
   K

Why should we weep because, as children of wit and folly formed out of inanimate dust, we are permitted to eat and drink and make love but for so fugitive a period? We have our hour for inventing " clay scarecrows " : who can hope to reverse the order of the hasting months or stay the sequence of day and night?

> " O God, although through fear I hardly dare
> To hint it, all the trouble springs from Thee !
> Hast Thou no sand or gravel in Thy sandals ? "

Parted from our darlings we must be. It is an ordinance older than the Milky Way.

> " What is this world ? What asken men to have ?
> Now with his love, now in the colde grave
> Alone, withouten any company."

The true achievement of the poetic imagination is to illuminate the transitory, " to see a world in a grain of sand," and to sing like a blackcap on a bramble !

> " A moment's Halt—a momentary taste
> Of Being from the Well amid the waste—
> And lo !—the phantom caravan has reach'd
> The Nothing it set out from—oh make haste ! "

Edward Fitzgerald I have every reason to praise ; his mantle has literally fallen upon my shoulders. In three continents my back has been warmed by his celebrated plaid shawl. It came through my uncle Mowbray Donne, the son of the " Old Donne "

of Fitzgerald's letters, and I have never been
oblivious of the honour chance thus bestowed on me.
Yet as I esteem Omar Khayyám and yet carp at him,
so do I esteem and yet grudge at his famous interpreter. For despite the apparent grace of Fitzgerald's quatrains, plaintive as the twittering of
migrating birds in the reeds of the Aldeburgh river,
I cannot reconcile myself to the lack of gusto
towards life that they display. In his letters this
prevailing mood is shown clearly—sad, mild, unim-
passioned.

> " June over ! A thing I think of with Omar-
> like sorrow. And the roses here are blowing—
> and going—as abundantly as ever in Persia."

Fitzgerald celebrates Love, Wine, and Poetry, but
ah ! how wanly. The faint desolation evoked by
these verses ill befits the poignant and profound
subjects of which they treat. Small wonder his
poem appealed to the Pre-Raphaelite group who had
accustomed themselves to see life always in reflection
like so many Ladies of Shalott ; even Swinburne,
if not writing of the sea, presenting us with a literary
shadowland in the place of Nature—a shadowland
where all is unreal, and where no cow-pats ever fell
plop upon an actual green earth.

Fitzgerald's interest in Omar was, indeed, scarcely
more than an indolent diversion to keep away " the
blue devils " of whom he so constantly complains.
There is upon occasion a disquieting suggestion

of an uneasy conscience over what he is about, so
hard is it for this old-fashioned Suffolk gentleman to
escape from the spiritual imprisonments of his time.

" The philosophy," he writes, referring to Omar's
poems, "is alas ! one that never fails in the world,"
and again, as though a kind of apology were demanded
of him, " No one cares for such things, and there are
doubtless so many better things to care about." This
proud reserved friend of Thackeray and Tennyson
could never have followed the advice of his great
Master, " Suppose thyself to be nothing and be free."
His boldest action, if we omit his separation from his
wife (and this was in keeping with the conduct of a
wealthy idiosyncratic bachelor who did not care to
alter his ways), was to dig up with Thomas Carlyle
the bones of the soldiers who fell at Naseby, the
battlefield being part of the Fitzgerald family
property.

An air of condescension mars his letters. This is
well illustrated by the absurd name he gave to the
fisherman for whom he had so romantic an attachment—and how could he be so banal as to allude to
Omar Khayyám as the " old sinner " ? It is true
that we have happier glimpses of him, as, for
example, when he was reading a copy of the wonderful
Bodleian Rubáiyát " profusely powdered with gold,"
in a Bedfordshire buttercup-filled horse-paddock
" brushed by a delicious breeze," and yet even in
these harmonious surroundings he displays the same
diffidence. " You would be sorry, too, to think that

Omar breathes a sort of consolation to me!"
These quiet scenes do have, however, a peculiar
grace of their own, similar to the gentle benediction
that used to come to Fitzgerald as he listened to the
Sunday hymn-singing from the field outside the
church of Boulge.

He now lies in the yard of that same Suffolk church
with the words " It is He that hath made us " to be
read on his gravestone. I myself have seen how
peacefully the sunlight falls upon that large field
which separates the church from the lane. The
landscape is a typically English one—a landscape of
calm and solid security, a landscape of white gates,
of white geese, and narrow daisy-white footpaths.

How different from the resting-place of the older,
tougher-hearted master! At the hour before dawn
the caravans approach Nishapour.

> " They feel the cool wet turf under their feet
> By the stream-side, after the dusty lanes
> In which they have toil'd all night."

The last stage of the travelling is almost over; the
drovers, trudging by the sides of their beasts, jest
under the cold stars, all of them heartless realists
with their heads full of thoughts that have more to
do with victuals and girls in the bazaars than with
God.

> " Wake ! For the Sun, who scattered into flight
> The stars before him from the Field of night
> Drives Night along with them from Heav'n, and strikes
> The Sultán's Turret with a shaft of Light."

It is daylight before the traders reach the city. They pass close to the tomb of Omar enclosed now in a seventeenth-century garden shrine put up by Shah Abbas the Great to the memory of Mohamed Mahruk. The camels, with their silent cushion feet, plod on, their grotesque antique faces snuffing up the air for the first whiff of anticipated fodder. The hungry men with quick black eyes observe every-thing—the scavenger dog they have disturbed, which, with long ribs showing, nervously raises a lank hind leg against a soiled wall, the fruit trees once more in blossom—a pear tree and a peach tree with petals falling on the poet's grave, as he had prophesied they would in the Slave Street eight hundred years ago.

The skull of Omar Khayyám must long since have fallen to pieces, a skull of dust that had once possessed a tongue of flesh. No emblematic coffin of vine-planks could long hold back from his " truth-speaking lips " their destined diet of sand. The heads of all men are but ephemeral pots of clay fitted with wagging tongues.

" Hear thou the word of Truth from Omar Khayyám
    Drink wine, rob on the highway, and be Benevolent."

Does this final admonition conceal an esoteric message for the freer spirits of every age? Though nearly a millennium has passed since " that great man has veiled his countenance in the dust," many still know themselves to be his natural children.

G. M. Powys.

NICCOLO MACHIAVELLI

NICCOLO MACHIAVELLI

IT is impossible for men to conduct themselves with consideration and control. The essential frivolity of their minds, the shallow inconstancy of their emotions, reveal on every occasion their base simian lineage. They are a breed of animals debarred by birth from civilized behaviour. With their close-set ears well plugged with Lucian's celebrated wax, the substance of which is ignorance and deceit; with their hearts full of "hidden malignity," they encompass the earth, generation after generation, the great in their pride, and the mob in their stench, without hope of improvement. Such were the "damnable opinions" of Machiavelli that for a period of four centuries have raised so noisy a clamour of dissension and protest.

What manner of man, then, was this Florentine Secretary, this "mokker of all religion and vertew"? Intellectual emancipation was as natural to him as was the air he breathed. The religious and ethical preconceptions that besot ordinary heads left his clear. It might be said that the grave import of the two words, good and evil, was never understood by him. As far as he was concerned, Eve might never have nibbled at her Venus pippin.

From a study of his work and of his private corre-
spondence it is easy to form an idea of the main
outlines of his philosophy. It was his fundamental
opinion that our life owes no single event to any
man-interested deity. He saw all earth-life carried
forward by an irresistible destiny, which, like an
insurgent flood, sweeps on and on to the unplumbed
ocean of death. But, as with the thought of
Epicurus, this Florentine Prometheus leaves a crack
open for the operation of man's free will. He held
that each of us has a modicum of freedom, an independent freehold, within the boundaries of which,
confined though they inevitably must be, foresight
and intelligent direction are still profitable; dykes
may be strengthened and banks thrown up against
the onrushing tidal wave. There can be in his
opinion no greater folly than for man to try to stem
the flood, to contest directly against the movement
of Fate. " I repeat once more, what from all
history is seen to be most true, that men may aid
Fortune, and not withstand her; they may weave
her webs but not break them."

His considered judgment of religion, that hoary
obsession of the nations, was completely cynical.
He regarded it merely as a providential instrument
of Government. " This good citizen," as Rousseau
called him, understood centuries before Karl Marx
its pragmatic use as a drug for the masses. To the
mystical claims of religion, so pathetic, indeed so
tragic, he remained, from first to last, blind, deaf,

and dumb.   In *The Prince*, his most perfect work,
precise and deadly as a poisoned dagger, he writes :—

> " To which end they [the Government]
> should countenance and further whatsoever
> tells in favour of religion, even should they think
> it untrue; and the wiser they are and the better
> they are acquainted with natural causes, the
> more ought they to do so."

To be " acquainted with natural causes "—that is
the open secret that should be the natural possession
of all free, practical spirits of *virtu*.   Life as he had
seen it in Renaissance Italy had destroyed his confidence in the efficacy of prayer.   He regarded
prayer as an entirely meaningless and fu+ile practice
inadvertently profitable to Governments, and that
was all.

> " Prayers are indeed necessary; and he is
> downright mad who forbids the people their
> ceremonies and devotions.   For from them it
> seems that men reap union and good order,
> and upon these depend prosperity and happi-
> ness.   Yet let no man be so silly as to believe
> that, if his house falls upon his head, God will
> save it without any other prop, for he will die
> beneath the ruins."

All his famous " policies " have their roots in his
indurated conviction as to the irremediable de-
pravity of mankind—" ungrateful, inconstant, hypocritical, fearful of danger, and covetous of gain."
This conviction is an accepted axiom with him, a

self-evident truth, and upon it he elaborates his subtle science. Anticipating our modern psychologists, he recognizes that morality is nothing but conduct-pressure from the herd.

> " The sanction of conduct was derived from positive institutions; where no law existed, no action could be unjust. . . . In the beginning of the world, as the inhabitants were few, they lived for a time dispersed after the manner of wild beasts, afterwards, when they increased and multiplied, they united together and in order the better to defend themselves, they began to look to that man among them who was the strongest and bravest, and obeyed him. From this arose the knowledge of the honourable and good, as opposed to things pernicious and evil."

It was thus that men came to know good and evil, but they remained still in their natures essentially brutish. " For men will always prove bad, unless by necessity they are compelled to be good."

There are two methods by which such necessary discipline can be applied : law and force. Of these the first is " proper to man," the second proper to beasts. " It belongs therefore to a Prince to understand both, when to make use of the rational and when of the brutal way." Fear rules the world. Fear is a more constant force and more to be relied upon than love.

> " Men have less scruple in offending one who is beloved than one who is feared : for love is

preserved by the bond of obligation, which, owing to the baseness of men, is broken at every opportunity for their own advantage; but fear is preserved by the dread of punishment, which never fails."

When once any society has been so drilled into good behaviour that the majority can live securely, there will be no more talk of freedom. " Justice embodied in Laws is the soul of Freedom."

He sees all states caught in a revolving wheel of inevitable recurrence.

> " *Virtu* produces peace, peace idleness, idleness disorder, disorder ruin . . . then when a district has been involved in disorder for a time, *virtu* returns to dwell there once again . . . for this is the circle revolving within which all states are and have been governed."

A hypocritical unction, a congenital leaning towards sanctimonious prevarication, is part of the very constitution of ordinary human beings. Machiavelli is himself entirely free of any such weakness. His mind is without cant. It strikes deep into life, as a man with a single stroke might stab at the bowels of his enemy. Continually he shocks our complacence, and indeed we may take it for granted that the traditional gregarious pre-possessions of our kind, their more tender superstitions, cannot have meant much to a man capable of alluding to Cæsar Borgia's murder of Vitellozzo and Oliverotto as the most beautiful treachery, " il bellissimo inganno " ! With his inhuman detachment he draws deductions from the affairs of men, as a vivisectionist might from the behaviour of his unlucky mice. He searches to deduce rules of conduct that are dependent upon " natural causes " and uninfluenced by human sentiment. His " Hatch-evil " writings are charged with dangerous non-moral dynamite. Perfidy, for example, deliberately used for a particular end, never struck him as dis-creditable, " for though the act accuses him, the result excuses him." Again and again he emphasizes the fact that people are always taken in by the " appearance and events of things," and he calmly announces that " he who is dead cannot think about revenging himself."

We can hardly wonder that *The Prince*, with its " pestilent Machiavellian policies," has been the treasured handbook of those who have aspired to tyrannical rule. It was the favourite night-cap reading of Louis XIV. Frederick the Great at-tempted to cover his dubious tracks by writing a treatise against it. A carefully annotated copy of it was found in Napoleon's coach at Waterloo.

Machiavelli observed that men shrink from leaving the beaten highway of human conduct, they do not dare to be " gloriously wicked " or, as he expresses it in his own reserved and sinister manner, " to have recourse to extremities." " The night that Pier Sodernini died his soul went down to the mouth of hell; but Pluto cried ' Foolish soul, no hell for thee. Go to the Limbo of the babes.' "

Cardinal Pole accused him of writing with the
finger of Satan, but in reality his pages are penned
with the cold starfish thumb of science.   He tells us
himself that he does not wish to give us a fancy
picture, but to go to the " real truth of things."   He
considers the problems of statecraft as though human
beings were beasts without hearts and as easy as
beasts to be overreached.   Throughout the generations idealists have always hated him, execrated
him, called him " illiterate atheist."   His unemotional conclusions have, however, appealed to
men of a scientific temper of mind, to men of reason,
like Bacon, who asserts : " We are much beholden
to Machiavelli . . . who wrote what men do and not
what they ought to do."

We would have gravely misunderstood Machiavelli nevertheless if we believed that the chiefest
interest of his years lay in the solutions of fine social
conundrums.   Though without doubt he recognized
the pleasure to be derived from " power acquired
and enjoyed on earth," yet the allegiance to life of
this great realist was too passionate, too imaginative,
too profound, to allow him to find his highest satis-
faction in such vanities.   It was natural for his mind
to be exercised with each succeeding political crisis,
but his secret preoccupation, his serious personal
preoccupation, was with his own love affairs.   There
is no doubt that these were the events that really
mattered to him.   Because La Barbere does not
write to him from Rome he takes no less a person

L

than Guicciardini into his confidence, and even
manages to persuade him to go and find out what
the matter is, " for she gives me more anxiety than
the Emperor himself." He dreads lest his reputation as a man of judgment may not be sufficient to
win for him " a fleeting kiss " from La Riccia, or
that age may deprive him of his privileged place by
Donato's fireside. It has often been so with great
men. It is always the conventional or the cabined
spirits who have turned away from this creative
source of recurrent animal refreshment. In one of
his letters Machiavelli declares that while his worldly
activities have brought him nothing but anxiety and
loss, from his love affairs he has derived in every case
advantage and joy.

In his late middle life, after he had been put upon
the rack and banished from Florence, it was still
this same sweet folly that sustained his soul. A
letter to his friend Francesco Vettori, a letter without
cynicism, sensitive, innocent even, has to do with a
girl he had met in the fields.

> " Being exiled in the country I have met with
> a creature so gentle, so delicate, so noble, both
> in her nature and her attributes, that I can
> neither praise nor love her as she deserves . . .
> the threads have become strong, made fast with
> knots that cannot be untied."

In a still more celebrated letter he describes his
daily life at San Casciano. In the morning he talks
with the woodcutters, " who are always full of some

misfortune either of their own or their neighbours ";
he then goes off to snare thrushes; and afterwards
to the tavern to play at cards or dice with the
butcher and miller and maltster, their voices sounding
far across the fields with " endless wrangling and
offensive words " over a disputed farthing.

> " The Brewer, the Maltster, the Miller, and I
> Left a heifer, left a filly, left a Ding Dong;
> They weren't the same pretties, but what's that to we,
> Pass along, boys ! Pass along ! "

And then in the evening he returns to his home,
and taking off his soiled country dress, he puts on
court attire and enters his library to commune with
the great minds of antiquity, a peer amongst his
peers, at peace at last, " and for the space of four
hours I feel no weariness, and forget every trouble;
I have no fear of poverty, and am not dismayed by
death."

A discerning reader may derive from his writings
certain invaluable hints as to the conduct of life.
His shrewd observations last well. " Honest slaves
are always slaves and good men always paupers."
He maintained that the secret of a fortunate life
lies in a man's power to adapt himself to the circumstances that are beyond his control, that man being
happy " whose manner of proceeding concerts with
the times, and he unhappy who cannot accommodate
to this." Above all things it is necessary to be
detached in one's outlook, to preserve always an
uninvaded philosophical citadel amid the jolting

events of this naughty world. " It is convenient
for his mind to be at his command and flexible to all
the puffs and variations of fortune." A man must
be ready at all times to return undistracted to the
hushed closet of his own proud, lonely soul. " For
long I have never said what I believed nor believed
what I said, and even if at times I speak the truth I
hide it among so many lies that it is hard to find."

Machiavelli was a liberal humanist, a spirited
advocate of the wisest and sanest of all human
traditions. In matters of love, wherein is man's
greatest profit under the sun, he forestalls the
wisdom of William Blake.

> " Those are tormented by Love who, when he
> settles in their breasts, would either bind him,
> or clip his wings. . . . But those who, when he
> goes let him depart, and when he returns accept
> him readily, are always honoured and caressed
> by him and triumph beneath his rule."

Upon our sad earth, where, because of false values
too readily accepted, where, because of thwartings
and frustrations, " men come to carry written in
their eyes the terror of their souls," few dare to speak
out the simple truth. To enjoy the present benefit
of time was Machiavelli's aim, and without reservations he exhorts us also to go and do likewise.

> " He who is held wise by day will never be
> held foolish by night; for he who is esteemed a
> man of worth, and who deserves such a reputa-
> tion, may do what he will to amuse himself and

to live gladly. . . . I can only give you this advice—to follow Love *totis habenis*, and that pleasure which you take to-day you will not have to take to-morrow. I beg of you to follow your star, and not to lose aught of what it may bring you for anything in the world; for I believe and always shall believe in the truth of what Boccaccio says : that 'it is better to do and to repent than not to do and to repent' . . . and thus we dally with these universal pleasures, enjoying what remains to us of this life, which seems to me a dream."

G. M. Powys.

FRANÇOIS RABELAIS

FRANÇOIS RABELAIS

RABELAIS'S genius is as deep and as uncircum-
scribed as is life. Here is a wild duck that will
support no saddle, a Bridle-goose not easily to be
bridled! For nearly four hundred years the wisest
scholars of Europe have tried to discover Rabelais's
secret and to explain it in words that all men could
understand. They have failed. Like Shakespeare
and like Goethe, he is an interpreter of the eternal
mysteries, and for this very reason is full of con-
tradictions. He is heretical, blasphemous, and yet
at the same time religious. He is gross, and yet at
the same time most delicate. To regard him merely
as a drinker with a taste for wenching is to mis-
understand the whole temper of his mind.

It is impossible not to be struck by the difference
between the Rabelaisian tone in regard to erotic and
excremental matters and the kind of outspokenness
of our own day. With Mr. James Joyce, for example, the urge underlying his obscenities is a
savage, almost pathological attraction-repulsion;
whereas with Rabelais " these primordials " simply
fall into their places like splendid sacraments,
essential parts of his huge gala song.

His broad, free, humorous treatment of " country

matters " has done us service. It has cleared the
air of much that is hypocritical and unseemly, and
has been a justification for many sincere people
who have wished to approach such subjects in a
natural way. It should be clearly understood that
Rabelais never wrote a single page that is porno-
graphic. In fact he is the great purifier. He lets
fresh air into the unhealthy closets of human
society, and his laughter, like sunshine, causes worm-
wood and pungent camomile to grow out of the
very middens of the world. Concealed drains are
dangerous, those open to the air harmless. Rabelais
follows the aristocratic tradition of *natural refinement*.

It is, in truth, Rabelais's wisdom to accept life
on its own terms. He is a philosophic optimist,
one of the few who commands our respect. Big
fish eat little fish, and he knows it well; but when
Panurge by his superior wit overreaches Ding-dong
and drowns sheep and shepherds in the sea, he feels
no concern. He is a true individualist and believes
that each human being should fulfil his destiny without let or hindrance. He is the champion of freedom, the liberator of the human spirit, and before
his God-like hilarity the conventions tremble.

As we read, however, it becomes clear that his
celebrated admonition " Do what thou wilt " resulted from his life-long conviction that constraint
and tyranny turn men's minds to evil. " Because
men that are free, well-born, well-bred, and con-
versant in honest companies, have naturally an

instinct and spur that prompteth them unto virtuous actions, and withdraws them from vice,"
Rabelais would have us feel confidence in the
natural goodness of man guided by the recom-
mendations of sweet reason. What he hates are
the narrow, unenlightened views of illiberal persons
who are forever trying to capture the wild gods
that they may domesticate them for their own
glory. Self-expression alone is of importance.
" Give yourself up to the study of Nature's truths
and let nothing in the world be unknown to you."
He would have each of us drink of the good wine
of life " with unbuttoned bellies."

He is contemptuous of those who sacrifice the
golden hours of consciousness to the task of making
money. When Pantagruel is asked to become
president of the courts, he refuses. " For," said
he, " there is too much slavery in these offices."
And later when Pantagruel offers Panurge " a sweet
remonstrance against his squandering the revenues
of the Lairdship of Salmygondin in Dipsodie " and
reminds him that his reckless manner of living
renders it " hugely difficult " for him (Pantagruel)
to make him rich, Panurge answers :—

> " Rich ! Have you fixed your thoughts
> there ? . . . Set your mind to live merrily in
> the name of God and good folks, let no other
> cark nor care be harboured within the sacro-
> sanctified domicile of your celestial brain. . . .
> For if you live joyful, merry, jocund, and glad, I
> cannot be but rich enough."

Apart from such honest harmless " knacks of wit," what wisdom is to be found in these extra-ordinary and fabulous chapters ! If the teaching of this " new gospel " had been followed for the last four hundred years, how large an amount of misery would the world have been spared ! This, for example, is how Rabelais writes of war :—

> " The time is not now, as formerly, to con-quer the kingdoms of our neighbour princes, and to build up our own greatness upon the loss of our nearest Christian brother. This imitation of the ancient Herculeses, Alex-anders, Hannibals, Scipios, Cæsars, and other such heroes, is quite contrary to the profession of the gospel of Christ . . . and that which heretofore the Barbarians and Saracens called prowess and valour, we now call robbing, thievery, and wickedness."

And again :—

> " These devilish kings, which we have here, are but as so many calves, they know nothing, and are good for nothing, but to do a thousand mischiefs to their poor subjects, and to trouble all the world with war for their unjust and detestable pleasure."

The style of this notable jester frisks and capers " like an ass with a brizze or gad bee under his tail." It is capable of scattering the vapours of all men, whether simple or learned. Not one of us but can play at his parlour games—at " charming the hare," at " grapple my lady." His high spirits redeem the most grotesque incidents. When Gargantua returns from war, he combs cannon-balls out of his hair, " which his father, Grangousier, seeing, thought they had been lice, and said unto him : ' What, my dear son, hast thou brought us this far, some short-winged hawks of the college of Montague? ' " Friar John is advised that the doctors think not too well of the excessive consumption of alcohol. " Well physicked," said the monk; " a hundred devils leap into my body, if there be not more old drunkards than old physicians." Panurge harbours a very characteristic grudge against the Parisians. " They are," said he, " little tippling sippers that drink no more than the little bird called a spink or chaffinch," and he loves nothing better than to see " a great puffguts of a counsellor " overthrown by his roguery. Epistemon, when he returned from his visit to hell (where he saw Xerxes, as a crier of mustard, and Villon, wrangling with him because he offered to enhance its price), brought back the comfortable news that the very devils were " boon companions and merry fellows." Whether in heaven or in hell, all is heyday with Rabelais. How excellent is the description of Panurge's dream !

> " A pretty, fair, young, gallant, handsome woman, who no less lovingly and kindly treated and entertained me, hugged, cherished, cockered, dandled, and made much of me, as if I had been another neat dilli-darling minion like Adonis.

. . . A little after, though I know not how, I thought I was transformed into a tabor and she into a chough or madge-howlet."

In his waking hours this most lovable wag of mediæval mischief and piety goes to the death-bed of the poet Raminagrobis, who has just driven from his chamber a flock of priests "dun and ash coloured," in order that he may be able to repose himself "and acquiesce in the contemplation of the vision, yea, almost in the very touch and taste of the happiness and felicity which the good God hath prepared for his faithful saints and elect in the other life and state of immortality." Though the old man was obviously dying "within grace," he was to Panurge, because he had offended the priest-hood, an arrant heretic "by the virtue of God, a resolute, formal heretic." Panurge was convinced his chamber was full of devils. He would not enter it again. "For," said he, "who knows but that these hungry, mad devils may in the haste of their rage and fury of their impatience, take a qui for a quo, and instead of Raminagrobis snatch up poor Panurge frank and free?"

It is interesting to notice as we read these broad pages the peculiar dignity, so natural and yet so spacious, that surrounds the lives of the giant kings. Their simplest actions have about them a grave and royal style, their great heads, large enough to contain whole worlds, are entirely purged of the kind of distempers that poison the minds of

men " who always look out at one hole." What
excellent reading it is when Grangousier catches
sight of the staff of one of the pilgrims that Gargantua is about to eat up with his lettuce, and
with true paternal care stays him for the moment
with the words, " I think that is the horn of a shell-
snail, do not eat it," or, best of all the glimpses
Rabelais gives us of the old king in his home when
" after supper he sits warming his ballocks by a
good, clear, great fire, and, waiting upon the broil-
ing of some chestnuts, is very anxious in drawing
scratches on the hearth, with a stick burnt at one
end, wherewith they did stir up the fire, telling to his
wife and the rest of his family pleasant old stories
and tales of former times."

When limited people deplore the works of Rabelais for religion's sake " my soul is ready to fly into
some marsh among frogs." That he was profoundly
religious can be proved in sentence after sentence.
Often in the midst of his maddest sallies, his most
copious ribaldry, there will fall upon the page a
sudden stillness, and this little great good man by
some utterance full of devout feeling will call up
comfort for our souls out of the depths. It has
been well said " he preserved a certain faith in
things that were for the time impossible of demon-
stration." Where you least look for it there starts
the hare. It appears that this doctor " in the
jovial quirks of his gay learning " *puts his trust in
God*. " Wisdom," he writes somewhere, " cannot

M

enter a malicious spirit, and knowledge without conscience is the ruin of the soul." Friar John declares against the priests, " But may God be their aid if they pray for us, and not through fear of losing their rich soups." To which Pantagruel answers, " All true Christians of all estates, in all places, in all times, pray to God, and the spirit prayeth and intercedeth for them, and God receiveth them into favour." Of great chapters in literature few are more moving than the one in which Pantagruel explains that the proclamation " the great God Pan was dead," delivered to the pilot Thamous in the Sea of Paxos, referred to the death of our Lord. It is a passage I would commend to the notice of all readers " who are worthy and fit to receive the celestial manna of honest literature." It is as though the pathos of that enchantment with which we surround our childish hopes were at last understood by a mind sensitive, undaunted, and full of a tender irony.

" For my part, I understand it of that great Saviour of the faithful who was shamefully put to death at Jerusalem. . . . And methinks my interpretation is not improper; for he may lawfully be said in the Greek tongue to be Pan, since he is our all. For all we are, all that we love, all that we have, all that we hope, is him, by him, from him, and in him. He is the God Pan, the great shepherd. At his death, complaints, sighs, fears, and lamentations were spread through the whole fabric of the universe, whether heaven, land, sea, or hell. . . . Panta-

gruel having ended this discourse remained
silent, and full of contemplation.   A little while
after, we saw the tears flow out of his eyes as
big as ostrich's eggs."

It has been my custom when in the presence of a
wise man to question him on the subject of the
immortality of the soul, and the answers I have got
have been "not unlike to the song of Gammer
Yea-by-nay."

No words uttered by Saint Paul are as apt at
allaying incredulity as are Rabelais's careless oracles.
" I believe," said Pantagruel, " that all intellectual
souls are exempted from Atropos's scissors."

The benedictions of Rabelais in their amplitude
resemble the benisons of the earth herself, as if the
corn-bearing, grape-bearing planet had blest us
with her wild blessing.   No man or no woman need
fear to go to confession "under a burdock leaf "
with such a monk.   He is the great reconciler of
the natural with the supernatural.   Catholics, Pro-
testants, Turks, and Atheists, we need none of us
feel ashamed to call ourselves believers after the
order of this Saint Francis Rabelais.   The net of
this antic fisher is wide and the meshes of it are free
and open.   " Now, my friends, you may depart,
and may that intellectual sphere, whose centre is
everywhere, and circumference nowhere, whom we
call God, keep you in his almighty protection."

G. M. Powys.

THOMAS DELONEY

THOMAS DELONEY

In English literature no great writer has been more neglected than has Thomas Deloney, the Elizabethan novelist. His three prose works, *Jacke of Newberie*, *The Gentle Craft*, and *Thomas of Reading*, have often enough been made centres of discussion by academic critics concerned to trace the origin and development of English prose fiction, but among the authors of all this scholarly research, there has been found no one to do adequate justice to his astonishing genius.

Outside of Christopher Marlowe, Shakespeare, Ford, and Ben Jonson, he has no match in the Elizabethan era. It is impossible for Thomas Deloney to write in a dull manner. His zest for life, quick as a sprite in a buttery, displays itself in every sentence, in every word that he puts down. His realism has never been equalled. His power in this kind is as sure as ever was that of Boccaccio. The characters he invents are no book characters. They are actual shop-door, street-corner people who eat possets, drink sack or muskadine, and cry, and sneeze, and stand upon very shoe-leather.

His affirmation of the delight of being abroad in the ordinary common-sense world is very stout. To contemplate a dame " carrying the keys of her cubberts gingling at her side " is for him reward enough. These three works might have been written by Sancho Panza, with such shrewd earth-aplomb do they present the impulses and the emotions of the indiscriminate crowd, of that section of the population which may be said to have their heads " screwed on the right way." Deloney's writing is never far removed from the dust of the King's High Road, from the egg-cobbles of the London streets, from actuality at its lowest level.

It has been a fanciful prejudice with me to remark a difference between flower-shop salesmen and iron-mongers. The former, because it is their profession to make commercial profit out of beauty, grow, so it seems, shallow and artificial in their address, whereas ironmongers, because it is their business to supply people with utensils necessary for daily use, become sensible and honest citizens. Thomas Deloney may be said to represent the ironmongers in literature ; one who knows how essential colanders, kettles, frying-pans, and saucepans are to human beings. The unredeemed lives of ordinary people are his province. His sense of poetry is of that simple kind that can be understood by everybody—by the coal-man, by the ice-man, by the fruit-man at the curb; the poetry that has to do with the yellow sun shining bright upon field and market-place, the poetry that has to do with the rumour that " women are not angels, though they have

angel faces "—the poetry, in fact, that is concerned
with the whole torrential stream of life, parti-
coloured, manifold with its sudden turns of fate,
turns of fate that overtake and surprise each one
of us with their irrelevant unexpectedness. And
what an observation Deloney had for the twists
and quirks to be found in human character! Carelessly he etches in for us brabbling dames, penny-
father old men, and prodigal youths; and at once
these phantom puppets of his imagination are walking between the street booths, standing at their
cutting-stools, or sitting at their removable refectory
tables gutting pudding pies; are actually there
before us, at one moment out of temper, and at the
next grinning, but always there firmly set in farting
flesh.

No lover of the sun should be content to remain
unacquainted with the prose works of this master.
" Yes, by Saint Anne, and ginger shall be hot i'
the mouth too." He is kin to Cervantes, sib to
François Rabelais. He belongs to those who do not
trouble themselves with the idealistic foibles that
besot the minds of so many human beings, to those
who are satisfied with the world as it is, with that
unregenerate world that wags on irrespective of
beliefs, in taverns where reckonings are " set up in
very fair chalk," and under the big elm trees in the
square where the butter-women's tongues " like
lambs' tails seldom stand still."

Thomas Deloney is not concerned with improving

manners or with inculcating moral precepts. His
vitality is such that he is able to celebrate every
phase of life. He is in love with the whole of life,
and his prodigious animal spirits make every object
he sees, every person he meets, interesting to him.
He has no desire to correct. He seems to take for
granted that his art could have no better purpose
than to present the great Shrove-Tuesday Procession
of life as it is, without comment.

Little is known about him. Nash refers to him
as " the Balletting Silke Weaver of Norwich," and
it has been assumed from his name that he belonged
to some continental Protestant family which,
because of religious persecution, had settled in
England. It was natural enough that the " university wits " should deride the work of " T. D.,"
for when they wrote of the underworld, it was from
above downward. To them Deloney was little
better than " a base mechanical." He had sold his
own ballads in Cheapside and sung them outside
countless alehouse doors. All his life long, appren-
tices, tradespeople, porters, serving-wenches, had
been his companions. He could write of Jack of
Newbury with enthusiasm because he himself had
not seldom been pinched of his victuals. He had
the poor man's romantic admiration for the rich
man's liberality because he had learnt how hard it
is to come honestly by a gammon of bacon. His
literary material is ever where human life is natural,
without pretensions. It never would enter the head

of a labourer going through the streets of a city to worry whether his hands were dirty, or whether the knees of his trousers had been patched : on such points he is without care, and Deloney wrote with the enfranchisement of one of the lower classes too pressed by life's realities to trouble much about its niceties.

He is supposed to have been born in 1543, and he died around 1600. It was by his ballad-writing that he first won popularity amongst skylarking prentices, cockcrow ostlers, impecunious trades-people, water-men, fairfield chafferers, and the un-numbered sweaty-caps of his time. Some disaster, a fire, a hanging, would be in everybody's mouth, and immediately up would start T. D., " in his tawny coat," to commemorate the event in jigging verse.

    " Like to the fatal ominous Raven which tolls
      The sicke man's dirge within his hollow beake."

Some popular discontent would be abroad in " Merrie England," and sure enough before long would find expression in one of Deloney's ballads. In the famine year of 1596 his " Ballad on the Want of Corn " was written to such purpose that for some time the Mayor of London was " in search for T. D." The ballad represented Queen Elizabeth as speaking with her people " Dialogue-wise in a very fond and undecent sort." It may have been this particular happening that turned Deloney's attention to prose, for we know that he had a son to provide for at his weaver's home somewhere in the parish of St. Giles, Cripplegate.

He wrote carelessly, " composing as he goes i' the street," giving the populace, to draw them from their dumps, imaginary stories of lives similar to their own.   To do it was as easy as sop to Deloney, because he knew his subjects so well.   We need not look for " any matter of light value, curiously pen'd with pickt words or choice phrases, but a quaint and plain discourse best fitting matters of merriment."   The University wits, these masters of " pick't words," saw him doing better than they what they had been trying to do; and many were the flirts and frumps that used to float down to the groundling poet from the heights of their Euphues Parnassus.   Greene, apologizing that he should demean himself by writing his *Defence of Conny Catching*, says, " Such triviall trinkets and threadbare trash, had better seemed T. D. whose braines beaten to the yarking up of Ballades, might more lawfully have glaunst at the quaint conceites of conny-catching and crosse-biting."   " These fellows," says another, " are in every corner of cities and market Townes of the Realme singing and selling of ballads and pamphlets full of ribauldrie, and all scurrilous vanity, to the prophanation of God's name."

" The Muse of Thomas Deloney," wrote Nash, " from the first peeping foorth, hath stood at Livery

at an Alehouse wispe, never exceeding a penny a
quart, day or night, and this deare yeare, together
with the silencing of his looms, scarce that; he
being constrained to betake him to carded Ale."

Kempe appended a note to his *Nine Daies Wonder*
addressed " to the impudent generation of Ballad-
makers." In this note he declares :—

> " I have made a privy search, what private
> Jigmonger of your jolly number hath been the
> Author of these abominable Ballets written of
> me. I was told it was the great Ballad-maker
> T. D., alias Thomas Deloney. . . . But I was
> given to understand, your late general, Thomas,
> died poorly (as you all must do) and was
> honestly buried, which is much to be doubted
> of some of you."

How often in Shakespeare have we longed for
more talk from the country people, from his God's
idiots, and weasel-brained hedge rogues! The
pages of Deloney are packed with such unstudied
chatter, packed with kitchen wisdom. His is the
wisdom of a coffin-bearer meditating upon a life
that is over; the wisdom of old Gran Prat, the mid-
wife, slapping a new-born baby to life, and meditating upon its future of lust and hunger and piety;
the wisdom of a town-crier; of an aged priest; the
wisdom that belongs to men and women who have
been so jostled by the years that they can be surprised by nothing, with minds sharp, shrewd, and
disillusioned that hit the mark at the first jump.

" For cunning continueth when fortune fleeteth . . .
it is gone, farewell it." All those apt saws, broad
expressions of speech that are to us so refreshing,
like time-resistant, homespun patches from the
cloak of human wisdom, abound in these little-read
pages. It may be for their very outspokenness that
they have received such scant recognition. Always
Deloney is a " groundling " writing for " ground-
lings," and his unintellectual simplicities and gross-
ness may be an offence to the official appraisers of
literature who pass through life removed from too
close contact with the " rabblement " who sweep
their floors, make their fires, and roast their capons.
Anybody who is directly concerned, day in and day
out, with the mean employments indispensable to
human living cannot be utterly foolish. To be
entirely superficial, one must be safely removed
from scouring pans. When a woman is hemming
a nightgown or cooking a Christmas dinner, without
conscious effort an awareness of the realities of
existence presses in upon her, and the same thing
happens to a man who strikes an ox to the floor
in the shambles, or who spends the greater part of
an April day digging a grave.

Deloney's world is a world of tradesmen, of
fickle-headed tailors, of weavers who sit at their
looms " in a row "; of the people who, though not
invited to the banquet, scrabble for the ortes
behind pantry doors and then return home to sleep
in truckle-beds; of the boys who play at push-pin

in the streets; of the boys who go to carry water from the conduit; of the old women who pummel soiled linen at the bottom step of a stairway leading down to the Thames—indeed, of all poor people whom, as Deloney remarks with gentle irony, " God lightly blesseth with most children."

If ever he has occasion to refer to the gentry or nobility, it is as privileged, faery-land folk with gracious manners and " lily-white hands," with whom he and his fellows, fighting for " bitten apples," have little in common. The motive of his plots often enough is the same motive that is popular to-day in the cinematograph theatres—the industry of a simple and good character suddenly rewarded, out of all expectation, with riches, and whose generosity—Deloney's most highly esteemed virtue— remains still, under the changed circumstances, un- corrupted by the " slyding wealth of the world."

It is in the London of Queen Elizabeth that his whimsical, jocund, and matter-of-fact characters live and move and have their being; in that Lon- don whose houses were, for the most part, mediæval, and where the Mermaid Tavern, with its two side doors, the one opening into Friday and the other into Bread Street, was still present : at a time when half an hour's walk through any of the city gates, through Ludgate or Moorgate or Bishops- gate, would bring a man into the open country of reddle-bellied rams, of white-bonneted maids, of sweet-breathing, patient cows. To-day, not far

N

from Westminster Abbey, there is a street called
Tuttle Street. It marks the place of Tuttle fields
where was a meadow, famous in Deloney's time for
assignations, a meadow to which went, in the Gentle
Craft, the two " proper neat wenches " looking for
heartsease and thrift. This is the London of
Deloney's stories: the London of timbered house-
fronts, of peeked gables, of steep-tilted roofs shining with snow over which one might expect to see
witches flying astride upon broomsticks. It is the
London of the train bands; the London of the
prentice boys crying " Clubs," the London where
" souls' cakes " were baked for All-hallow-e'en; the
London resonant with the hearty calls of night-
watchmen, " Two of the clock and a cold and frosty
morning "; the London where lighted lanterns were
hung in the church steeples after dark for the help
of belated travellers; the London of cobble streets
and garbage litter; the London of enclosed tavern
yards, encircled with balconies, where, as the night
passed, the " anon Sir, anon, Sir " of the drawer
would imperceptibly give place to the stillness of
the dead hours, when the only sound was an
occasional stamp from tired horses, as King
Charles's Wain rose high and higher over the " new
chimney."

As it is so often with great artists, this " halfpenny
chronicler " created within the circle of this actual
Elizabethan London another London of his imagination, and this new London presently takes to itself

its own reality, a fabulous Rabelaisian reality under old St. Paul's.

> " Afterwards they proceeded, and came to Paules Church, whose steeple was so hie, that it seemed to pierce the cloudes, on the top whereof, was a great and mightie wether-cocke, of cleane silver, the which notwithstanding seemed as small as a sparrow to men's eyes, it stood so exceeding high, and which goodly weather cocke was afterwards stolen away, by a cunning cripple who found meanes one night to clime up to the top of the steeple, and tooke it downe."

Which of us has not been teased out of mind by a desire to have free entrance into the London of " Shakespeare's boys "? Ignorant we have of necessity remained. " We may as well push against Powles as stir 'em." It is all here for us in Deloney's work. To read these three novels is to be privy to the stir of those far-off, noisy alleys; it is to rub shoulders with these vigorous men and women, and to hear their exact speech, the very words of the formal burgomaster in his velvet cap, the very words of the man " well whitled " staggering by a red-latticed sill, the very " prittle prattle " of the drabs in the rain.

To read Thomas Deloney's novels for the first time is an unequalled experience. He himself boasted that they were " very fit to passe away the tediousness of the long winter evenings," and he never spoke a more true word. There is none who writes after his sort, so nimble, so solid, so

honest.   What a smack of ancient actuality has been
hidden away in these incomparable paragraphs !

Thomas Deloney defeats even Mortality.   The
prisoners that Death over three hundred years ago
herded out of Cheapside and Pudding Lane no longer
play at " mum budget," are no longer dumb.   Their
everyday canting talk comes to us pat across the
centuries, as if they themselves were " rounding us
in the ear."   For Thomas Deloney knew them as a
gamin knows his pennies.

> " Twittle, twattle I know what I know. . . .
> Life, why, what is it but a floure, a bubble in
> the water, a spann long and full of misere :
> and trust me I doe detest life, worse than a
> goat doth hate basil . . . with hey trickse,
> tringoe tricksee.   Under the greenwood tree."

G. M. Powys.

ROBERT BURTON

ROBERT BURTON

ROBERT BURTON was in my opinion the greatest prose-writer of the greatest age of prose-writing that England has seen. Fuller's glancing style, the silvery clearness of Izaak Walton, the studied assonance of Sir Thomas Browne—like echoes in charnel-house corridors with knuckle-bones for commas and skulls for periods—weigh light in comparison with the work of this " loose, plain, rude writer." The wisdom of this old Oxford don wears well. The passing of the years does not invalidate it.

Burton was no metaphysician. He was a philosopher in the old broad usage of that word. He brings all his learning, all his wide reading, all his celibate sagacity to bear upon the spectacle of human life upon earth. Left to " mine own domestic discontents " in his study at Christ Church, he finds himself in a strategical position for conning without sentimentality " this mart of walking spirits." He reviewed the motley temporal world from his vantage point of perdurable wisdom; and now from a position " common as a barber's chair," and now from " his college window," he

blows hot and cold upon the huge porringer of
life.

Though the old man has his fantasies, he is not
deceived about the facts upon which our existence is
built. The memory of death is never for long out
of his head. " 'Tis an inevitable chance, the first
statute in Magna Charta, an everlasting act of
Parliament." Here in the world, where " men
contend as fishes do for a crumb that falleth into
the water," where " commodity steers our affections
throughout," all things flow away. What matters
our strutting and becking and nodding?—" phan-
tastic shadows, gulls, monsters, giddy heads, butterflies !" " What's a thousand years to eternity . . .
innumerable, infinite millions of years, *in omne
ævum, in æternum*. O Eternity !" Burton sus-
pects life " as a fox on the ice." " We are all
prisoners. What is our life but a prison? We are
all imprisoned in an island. . . . Whatsoever is under
the moon is subject to corruption, alteration, and as
long as thou livest upon earth look not for other."
If it were allowed, it were well to alter it. " The
whole world belike should be new-moulded . . . and
turned inside out as we do haycocks in harvest."

The inveterate folly of the human mind causes
him more and more to marvel. " It were enough,"
he thinks, " to make them wise, if they would but
consider the mutability of the world and how it
wheels about, nothing being firm and sure. Never
so much cause of laughter as now, never so many

fools and mad-men." How many humours in man
—and to anatomize melancholy, what a task!
More difficult than to trace out all the bays and
sounds of the north-east passage "beyond the mighty
promontory of Tabin "!

Thought itself is to be suspected. Burton was of
opinion that "fools and dizzards live the merriest
lives." Yet his despondency was not, in its ultimate
analysis, an intellectual thing. "Saturn was lord
of my geniture." Melancholy covered him like an
old clout of dun or russet wool. Two influences
undoubtedly augmented this congenital mood—the
misery he suffered at his school, and the fact that
"Venus omitted, produceth like effects." This last
explains much, if not all. "They will by all means
quench their neighbour's house if it be on fire, but
that fire of lust which breaks out into such lamentable
flashes they will not take notice of." It explains
why he was constitutionally out of conceit with life,
and why, whenever he writes of anything that
has to do with "merry entertainment," his pen
prances.

It is in the nature of man to be satisfied easily.
If his hands and his emotions find expression, he is
under no pressure to use his head. Life acts as a
whetstone for our terraqueous and sottish wits.
We construct illusions and are content in shunning
unpalatable thoughts. It is only when things have
gone awry that, here and there, like thistles in corn,
people who use their minds see through the con-

ventional veils that human susceptibility is forever
hanging between themselves and reality. When eyes
are unblinkered, all grows unsteady as a cockboat
at sea. Against a firmament " of such incomparable
bigness as the Copernical giants will have it," all is
reduced to nought. " If it be so that the Earth is
a moon, then are we also giddy, vertiginous, and
lunatic within this sublunary maze . . . when all are
mad, who can discern madness? I refer to you,
though you be likewise fools and madmen, and I as
mad to ask the question."

Robert Burton was a person " of great honesty,
plain dealing, and charity . . . a modest man, a
generous spirit, one that hath grace," and, because
he could not himself remedy rampant evil, he
revenged himself by exposing it. He was not
easily taken in. Look where he might, he saw
nothing but rogues and bladder heads; " go back-
ward and forward; choose out of the whole pack,
' wink and choose, you shall find them all alike,
never a barrel better herring."

To this old scholar sitting in his chambers, sweet-
ened with burning juniper, the human scene became
a matter for laughter. He himself was outside the
scramble. " I have little. I want nothing; all my
treasure is in Minerva's tower." He no longer
bustles for preferment. These " trencher chaplains "
have always been too quick for him. He is not one
to go " crouching to a rich chuff for a meal's meat."
He is " like a mired horse that struggles at first . . .

but when he sees no remedy that his beating will not serve, lies still." On every side he saw men " besotted with their wealth as birds with hen-bane." Proud in his humility, " proud in that he is not proud," he lets the " griping patrons " and pompous " huffing bishops " go by. In the management of the earth neither honesty nor reason is in the ascendant, and a wise man can do nothing better than " set his hands to his sides and laugh profusely " at the ways of the world.

The manifest " wrongs and absurdities " are too gross for gravity—to see " a lamb executed, a wolf pronounce sentence," to see " a man smile with an intent to do mischief, or cozen him whom he salutes," to see " a wittol wink at his wife's honesty, and too perspicuous in all other affairs," to see a jealous husband " as a heron when she fishes, still prying on all sides . . . why did she smile . . . a whore, a whore, an arrant whore ! " to see a man " roll himself up like a snowball, from base beggary to right worshipful and right honourable titles . . . a hirsute beggar's brat, that lately fed on scraps, crept and whined, crying to all, and for an old jerkin ran of errands, now ruffle in silk and satin, bravely mounted, jovial and polite . . . insult over his betters."

By the contemplation of such a panopticon of whim-whams he seeks to restore those who suffer from melancholy. 'Tis a method of his own, a sort of spiritual homeopathy invented by this " wearish "

old empiric.   For he himself had " a kind of impos-
tume in his head."   True, his book is full of conceits
and contains not a dull page, but despite that it is so
frolic its import is grave.   He knew of what he was
speaking.   This surly humour and he had long been
bedfellows.   He writes of melancholy " by being
busie to avoid melancholy."   " If there is a hell on
earth it is to be found in a melancholy man's heart
. . . I say of our melancholy man, he is the cream
of human adversity, the quintessence, the upshot;
all other diseases whatsoever are but fleabitings."
Through the pages of his lifelong work he offers
himself as a scapegoat to posterity.   In his own
quaint way he says as much, " the great captain
Zisca would have a drum made of his skin when he
was dead, because he thought the very noise of it
would put his enemies to flight.   I doubt not but
the following lines . . . will drive away melancholy,
though I be gone."   And 'tis a brave drum he
bequeathed to us.   Many a dispirited eccentric has
been heartened by hearing the resonant tattoo,
now light, now heavy, on the skin of this tough
old ass.

What manner of man was Burton?   He only half
reveals himself even to those of his own kidney.
" You may as well make the moon a new coat " as
try to present him in his true character.   It is
happiest, perhaps, to think of him staying with his
mother in Leicestershire.   Much of the homely
power of his prose he got, it seems, from this country

background; for it is abundantly clear that he, the great worthy of Oxford, was not always in love with being "mewed up in cloisters," penned in "like a hide-bound calf in a pasture." There were occasions when he was in two minds to turn his philosopher's gown "into a miller's coat . . . to sell ale as some have done, or worse," being impatient with his case, "kept from his cradle to his old age to behold the same still, still, still the same, the same."

It was down at Lindley, that "ancient patrimony in our family," that he observed Dame Dorothy, his mother, apply "the amulet of a spider in a nutshell lapped in silk" for an ague. "I could see no warrant for it. *Quid aranea cum febre ?* For what antipathy? Till at length, rambling among authors (as often I do), I found the very medicine in Dioscorides, approved by Matthiolus, repeated by Alderovandus. *Cap. de Arenea, lib., de insectis.* I began to have a better opinion of it." We can well imagine him passing his days "in vacation" in that fat hunting country that had the praise for good "sydowe pease"; now talking with his brother, William, whose natural genius "had led him to the studies of heraldry, genealogies, and antiquities"; now sitting alone under the shade of boughs and leaves "plashed for cattle to stand under"; now walking in orchards and "back lanes" ; now in neat gardens "full of exotic, versicolour, diversely varied, sweet-smelling flowers"; now along the banks of the River Anker, looking about him "with

great delight " to see " herons, ducks, water-hens,
coots, and many other fowl, with their brood." Or
he would loiter, perhaps, through the village,
observing how a strange cur " if he clap his tail
between his legs " will provoke other dogs " to insult
over him," whereas, if he " bristle up himself and
stands to it none will meddle with him." With an
" ambient air," so health-giving, he could not but
have found sanctuary from melancholy, " that feral
fiend." He would sit down to a game of chess
with his brother George or sister Katherine, in
summer time " with roses, violets, sweet-smelling
flowers in the windows," or, in winter, close up
against the hearth " on cloudy, lowering, dark
days."

> " Chess-play is a good and witty exercise for
> the mind . . . but if it proceed from overmuch
> study it may do more harm than good; it is a
> game too troublesome for some men's brain, too
> full of anxiety, all but as bad as study; besides
> it is a testy, choleric game and very offensive
> to him that loseth the mate."

And then back again he would be in Oxford,
giving the sacrament in wafers in the parish of St.
Thomas and living " a silent, solitary, private life,
mihi et musis "; borrowing books from John Rouse,
the librarian of Sir Thomas Bodley's library—
Chaucer, Montaigne, Rabelais, Hakluyt—or at
some mellow midnight hour taking " a nutmeg and
ale, or a good draught of muscadine, with a toast and

nutmeg, or a posset of the same " with Mr. Whitehall,
" myne own Chamber Fellow."

We get odd and characteristic glimpses of him.
One day he was sitting in the corner of a bookshop
when the Earl of Southampton came in to bespeak
a copy of the *Anatomy*. The obsequious stationer
hastened to introduce the nobleman to the absent-
minded scholar. " ' Mr. Burton,' says the Earl,
' your servant.' ' Mr. Southampton,' says Mr.
Burton, ' your servant,' and away he went," his
head preoccupied with a thousand unexpected medi-
tations as he shambled off past The Mitre in his old,
torn gown, " ensign of his infelicity "; how the
whole of life " is an Irish Sea, wherein there is
nought to be expected but tempestuous storms . . .
say poor and say all "; how he already had been in
the university " as long, almost, as Xenocrates at
Athens "; how wearisome a thing college life was
—" leaping out of our beds when we hear the bell
ring, as if we heard a thunderclap " . . . and this,
when sleep " moistens and fattens the body as we
see in dormice . . . sleeping under the snow in the
dead of winter, as fat as butter." He would recall,
perhaps, how he had " stood stupefied many times "
at the first sight of beauty—before " the clear light
of the moon," or at a market maid crossing the road.
" Great Alexander married Roxane, a poor man's
child, only for her person. 'Twas well done of
Alexander, and heroically done. I admire him for
it." Then once more he would be caught up in his
o

old depression, " extreme lumpish again in an
instant . . . under hatches, dejected, rejected," as
his mind would drift with more envy toward the
skipping lechery of " afternoon men " and " how
many decrepit, hoary, harsh, writhen, busten-
bellied, crooked, toothless, bald, blear-eyed, im-
potent, rotten old men shall you see flickering still
in every place ? "

Yet the impression that Burton left behind was
not of a crabbed or malicious man. Evidently—
and we can well believe it in the intervals of his
vapours—he was a sly droll at the high table.
Anthony à Wood reported that he had heard
" some of the antients of Christ Church say
that his company was very merry, facete, and
juvenile."

In January of the year 1640 he faced the last
and greatest terror, *ultimum terribilium*. He died
on the very day that he himself had predicted by
the casting of his horoscope. It was whispered
through the festive halls of Oxford " that rather
than there should be a mistake in the calculation he
sent up his soul to Heaven through a slip about the
neck." It may be noted also that several years
later Mr. Robert Hooke told Aubrey that " he lay
in the chamber of Christ Church that was Mr.
Burton's, of whom 'tis whispered non obstante all
his astrology and his books of melancholy, that
he ended his days in that chamber by hanging
himself."

The epitaph he composed may still be read on his monument in Christ Church Cathedral. It is the scroll of " a polite and terse academic " such as he prided himself on being " Paucis notus, paucioribus ignotus, hic jacet Democritus Junior, cui vitam dedit, et mortem Melancholia."

G. M. Powys

THOMAS HOBBES

THOMAS HOBBES

As soon as ever settled societies gave human beings leisure for thought, their anxious minds began to attribute the management of the world to unseen powers. In the course of the millenniums these conclusions were taken for granted, and, wherever the earth was inhabited by man, spiritual yearnings were directed heavenward.

From time to time throughout the centuries there have appeared thinkers who have been inclined to believe that the universe is unswayed by moral considerations, and that man is " as a colt of a wild ass in a wilderness without owner or obligation." Amongst these philosophers, extending from Epicurus to Santayana, Thomas Hobbes holds an important place. Francis Bacon used to commend Machiavelli for treating of " what men do in fact, and not what they ought to do," and the youth from Malmesbury who would walk by his side along the fragrant terraces and plum-tree avenues of Gorhambury was destined still further to develop this realistic method so troubling to idealists of every age. Bacon used often to say that he " better liked Mr. Hobbes's taking his thoughts, than any of the others, because he understood what he wrote which the others not understanding, my Lord would many times have a hard task to make sense of what they writt." It is easy for us to believe this, for the sagacious champion of experimental physics—" a true Extender of the Kingdom of Man over the universe "—was likely enough to find an attentive and apt disciple in a young man who held religion to have its root in fear of the supernatural and society in the fear of man; and who in another thirty years was to be charged with judging " school learning no better than plain jargon, that is, senseless gibberish or a fustian language like the chattering noise of sabots." It is a fact that Hobbes never succeeded in dissociating Oxford and Cambridge from the traditional word-wisdom of the schoolmen. " If words alone were sufficient, a parrot might be taught as well to know truth as to speak it." He taunted these houses of official learning for their insignificance of speech. " The universities have been to the nation as the wooden horse was to the Trojans," and again, " All the haranguing of infinities is but the ambition of schoolboys." Homer and Virgil were amongst the books usually to be seen on Hobbes's table, but he was fond of telling people that " if he had read as much as other men, he should have known no more than other men," a brag noted by Voltaire, who drily says of the greatest of all English anti-clerical philosophers that he had read nothing " pas même l'Evangile."

Hobbes was of course a sound scholar and a highly

cultured man; but he may also be held up as an
example of the extraordinary value of unacademic
home-spun thinking. It was he who first boldly
wrote, " Know, then; that all this is but an empty
store of words, that has been drawn up and arraigned
against the senses." His philosophy was firmly
based on the most materialistic convictions, but
never was there a sage more adroit at imparting his
wisdom by implication rather than by direct utterance. That he was chary of giving to the world all
his philosophic conclusions may be gathered from
the remark he made after reading Spinoza's *Tractatus
Theologico-politicus*, " He has cut through me a bar's
length, for I durst not write so boldly."

The secret of all life's manifestations Hobbes
believed to be motion. It was the perpetual flux
of the Democritean atoms acting through the senses
on the dull organs of the body that caused the brain
to be disturbed into thought, as a rustling shiver
will pass through the leaves of a poplar tree at a
rising of the wind. He found, as others have found
before him, and as others will find in the future, that
the way of the senses is no way of error. The
Leviathan, and Hobbes's argument with Bishop
Bramhall, reveal him as a convinced determinist;
and seldom if ever has the case against free will been
treated with a firmer hand, or the case against
Catholicism been presented more trenchantly. It
is his humour in the last chapter of his famous work
to liken the papacy to the kingdom of the fairies.

His huge mind disports itself with this fancy like a midsummer bull in a field of buttercups. Very clear and vigorous is the peroration and most admirably is it enlivened.

> " The *ecclesiastics* are *spiritual* men, and *ghostly* fathers. The fairies are *spirits* and *ghosts*. *Fairies* and *ghosts* inhabit darkness, solitudes, and graves. The ecclesiastics walk in obscurity of doctrine, in monasteries, churches, and church-yards. . . . The *ecclesiastics* take from young men the use of reason, by certain charms compounded of metaphysics and miracles, and traditions, and abused Scripture, whereby they are good for nothing else, but to execute what they command them. The *fairies* likewise are said to take young children out of their cradles, and to change them into natural fools, which common people do therefore call elves, and are apt to mischief.
>
> " The *fairies* marry not; but there be amongst them *incubi*, that have copulation with flesh and blood. The *priests* also marry not."

Hobbes's interest in mathematics was but a late development, and it was possibly for this reason that his University opponents found it so easy to make game of his indiscretions. Provoked by Descartes's writings in favour of transubstantiation, " done merely to put a compliment on the Jesuits," he did not scruple to suggest that the philosopher should concentrate his entire attention upon geometry, seeing that his head " did not lie for

philosophy." After the same manner, he himself
had been wise to keep clear of higher mathematics,
seeing that it " laid him so open."

How absorbing is the life of Thomas Hobbes, how
solid, how idiosyncratic—and how long ! He was
born in the village of Westport just outside Malmesbury, in the year 1588, an April-Fool child, after
his mother had received the false news that the
Spanish Armada had come at last. Hobbes in after
years used to suspect that his premature arrival
disposed his nature to timorousness, a life-long
characteristic which was conspicuously displayed
upon the publication of his celebrated " little
treatise," so subversive to the pretensions of the
Parliament. " Then thought Mr. Hobbes, ' 'tis time
now for me to shift for myselfe,' and so withdrew
into France, and resided at Paris . . . the first of all
that fled." On the occasion of the publication of
Leviathan he once more felt himself to be in jeopardy,
and returned to England with a like alacrity,
duly proffering his submission to the Council of
State in 1652, and never again leaving his native
land. His foes tried to suggest that he had deliberately written *Leviathan* " in defence of Oliver's
title," and afterwards Clarendon repeated, as though
it were meant seriously, Hobbes's jesting reply to the
question of how he could publish such a doctrine—
" The truth is I have a mind to go home." Not
only was physical courage not possessed by Hobbes,
but it was not even highly respected by him. With

reluctance he concedes it to be " a royal virtue," but
" though it be necessary in such private men as shall
be soldiers, yet for other men, the less they dare, the
better it is both for the commonwealth and for
themselves."

It was because of his low opinion of the generality
—base, greedy, and quarrelsome—that Hobbes
defended the principles of arbitrary governments,
albeit the " trim commonwealth " he envisages,
founded neither upon religion towards God nor
justice towards men, was not likely to be pleasing
either to priests or to presbyters. There can be
no doubt that the philosopher judged human nature
to be so degraded that only the strictest discipline
could possibly serve its turn. He believed, however,
that society was in no real danger, even in the most
broken times, because its stability was established
in the firm soil of self-interest. " Hobbes," Descartes curtly declared, " held all men to be wicked
and gave them grounds for wickedness "; an attack
that received a century later a just reprisal from
Voltaire, who wrote of Descartes, " This best of
mathematicians made only romances in philosophy.
. . . It is given us to calculate, to weigh, to measure,
to observe, this is natural philosophy; almost all
the rest is chimera."

Hobbes was the son of one of the ignorant " Sir
Johns " of Queen Elizabeth's time. The old vicar
was a " good fellow," and it used to be said of him
that he would doze in his church on Sundays only to

wake suddenly with the cry " Trafells (clubs) is
troumps." Thomas Hobbes, because of his dark
hair, was nicknamed " Crow " at school. From the
first, he was independent in his ways. It was said
he was utterly careless of the official curriculum at
Oxford. He would go to the bookbinders' shops
and for hours together " lie gaping on mappes." As
private tutor to Lord Cavendish, son and heir of
the Earl of Devonshire, he almost forgot his Latin,
so much time did he spend in hunting and hawking
with his high-spirited pupil. Indeed, his reading of
the classics became confined to those brief intervals
when his charge visited the jakes upon his natural
occasions. The young nobleman was evidently a
spendthrift, for Aubrey tells us that one of Hobbes's
duties was to borrow money for him, and that he
Hobbes—in performing this task " took cold, being
wet in his feet (there were no hackney coaches to
stand in the street), and trod both his shoes aside
the same way." We may well believe that this
especial employment required the greatest tact, and
was even so a thankless one; for in after years
Hobbes himself wrote the following wise words:
" All men are by nature provided of notable multi-
plying glasses through which every little payment
appeareth a great grievance." Hobbes served three
generations of the Cavendish family, and grateful
indeed must all lovers of " humane learning " be to
this English house for sheltering the philosopher to
his great old age. There were, it is true, certain

intervals in his life when Hobbes lived without the
Devonshire patronage. For some time he was
travelling tutor to the son of Sir Gervase Clifton, and
until he was appointed mathematical tutor to the
Prince of Wales he lived in Paris, occupied with
" the meetings of learned men." Also on his return
to England he seems to have taken lodgings for a
time in Fetter Lane; but it was standing at the
gate of the third Earl of Devonshire's London resi-
dence, Little Salisbury House, that he was recognized by Charles II as he drove through London at
the time of the Restoration. This highly civilized
monarch bared his head to the old Falstaffian
monitor, calling him to his carriage door. Afterwards he gave him a pension of one hundred pounds,
hung his portrait up in the royal closet, and let it
be known that he should always be allowed free
access to the palace. The King used to take
pleasure in the old man's *bonhommie* wisdom, and
on seeing his familiar figure enter the state rooms
at Whitehall, would cry out, " Here comes the bear
to be baited," pleasuring himself much to hear the
young blades of fashion try to overreach the sagacious old man who would so often set the whole
Court laughing with his dextrous repartees. There
was a kind of childish innocence about Hobbes that
must have been very disarming. He was capable of
giving expression to the most outrageous views
without seeming to anticipate the tumult they would
be likely to arouse in limited minds. On his return

to Paris after the Battle of Worcester, Hobbes presented Charles with the copy of *Leviathan* " engrossed in vellum in a marvellus fair hand " still to be seen in the British Museum. The book had an ill reception. The attitude of the Church, with " its leg of gold and leg of an ass," may be somewhat recovered for us in the following extract from a contemporary letter :—

> " All honest men here are very glad that the King hath at length banished from the court that father of atheists Mr. Hobbes, who, it is said, hath rendered all the Queen's Court, and very many of the D. of York's family atheists, and if he had been suffered, would have done his best to have likewise poisoned the King's court."

Charles, as usual, seems to have placated the popular feeling and reserved his own private opinion, which in this case was without doubt correct. He was often heard to say that " he never thought Mr. Hobbes meant to do him harm."

During his stay in Paris, Hobbes won the affection and respect of most of the learned men of Europe. Years afterwards, when he visited England, the Grand Duke of Tuscany took away his portrait and his books to be preserved in the Medicean library. Galileo was his friend, and Gassendi, and the celebrated Franciscan Friar, Marin Mersenne. Edmund Waller told Aubrey that he remembered meeting Descartes and Hobbes at the table of the

P

Marquis of Newcastle.   It was about the time that
Hobbes had the one serious illness of his life and was
thought to be dying.   Mersenne hastened to his
bedside to assure him of the power of his Church
to remit sins.   " Father," Hobbes said, " I have
long gone over that question in my own mind.
You have something pleasanter to say.   When did
you see Gassendi? "   Aubrey reports that other
divines did not hesitate to press their way into his
chamber.   " Let me alone," the dying man is said
to have exclaimed, " or else I will detect all your
cheats from Aaron to yourselves."

" Here lies Tom Hobbes, the Bugbear of the Nation
  Whose death hath frightened Atheism out of fashion."

After the Plague and Fire of London a wave of
superstition spread over the country, and he who
had been called the crow of Malmesbury became the
scarecrow of England.   A Bill was presented to
Parliament for the suppression of Atheism and
blasphemy, and a committee was instructed by the
House of Commons to receive information about
" Mr. Hobbes's *Leviathan*."   Some of the Bishops
made a motion to have " the good old gentleman
burn't as a Heretique," and it was probably to the
friendliness of the Home Secretary, Arlington, and
to the good sense of the King, that Hobbes owed his
immunity, rather than to his own investigations into
the laws of heresy which culminated in an essay
vigorously proving that it would be an act of grossest

illegality to commit him to the flames. "So fierce are men, for the most part, in dispute, when either their learning or power is debated, that they never think of their laws, but as soon as they are offended, they cry out, crucifige." A man who considered imagination nothing but "decaying sense" would naturally be suspected of other doctrines fundamentally subversive to the accepted theology of the times. Hobbes had always held the dangerous belief that "Evidence is to truth as the sap to the trees," and he was constantly put to his shifts to exonerate his works from the charge of Atheism. To him spirits had either to be corporeal or non-existent.

This was an article of his faith quickly seized upon by his opponents. Bishop Bramhall pressed him so tight that Hobbes was fain to cross to safe theological ground on a bridge of split hairs. He had once observed that the mixing of river water with mineral water had resulted in a substance indistinguishable from milk.

> "If then such gross bodies have so great activity, what shall we think of spirits whose kinds be as many as there be kinds of liquor and activity greater? God therefore is not incorporeal but is only called so to indicate a mysterious essence that is 'something between infinitely subtile and nothing less subtile than infinitely subtile yet more subtile than a thought.'"

The contempt with which Hobbes regarded the

free-will notions of Bishop Bramhall and his other
Arminian opponents is well shown by his remark,
" Bramhall talks as if the will and the faculties were
men or spirits in men's bellies." In controversies
such as these he was well qualified to defend himself.
" Words are wise men's counters; they do but reckon
with them, they are the money of fools." As much,
however, cannot be said of his adventures in the
realms of mathematics.

> " He was 40 years old before he looked on
> geometry; which happened accidentally. Being
> in a gentleman's library in . . . Euclid's ele-
> ments lay open, and twas the 47 El libri 1.
> He read the proposition. ' By God,' sayd he,
> ' this is impossible ! ' So he read the demon-
> stration of it, which referred him back to such a
> proposition; which proposition he read. That
> referred him back to another, which he also read.
> *Et sic deinceps*, that at last he was demon-
> stratively convinced of the truth. This made
> him in love with geometry."

It was his belated passion for the " art diabolical "
that led him to boast that he had squared the circle.
He was unwise enough to insert a chapter in one of
his books of first principles in which he made a show
of his mathematical gifts. Immediately he found
that the wooden horse was within the walls of his
Troy town, and that his vaunting had involved him
in his humiliating wrangle with the time-serving
university turncoat geometrician, Dr. John Wallis of
Oxford. Well might Dr. John Fell say that " for a

man to begin to study mathematics at forty years old
'tis as if one should at that age learn to play on the
lute." But Hobbes, with the whole mathematical
world against him, remained undaunted. He con-
fessed that either he or they must be mad, but
between two such alternatives the answer seemed to
him clear as the day. For over twenty years the
controversy raged, the Oxford Don punctually
replying to each " Lesson for Oxford Professors "
that Hobbes cared to deliver. It was not till the
year 1676 that the quarrel closed with the unvan-
quishable veteran circle-squarer sending to the press
at the age of ninety a work entitled *Decameron
Physiologicum*. It is generally allowed that, in
spite of demonstrable errors of the grossest kind,
Hobbes showed that he possessed a remarkable grasp
of the general theory of mathematical reasoning.

The last years of his life were spent in Derbyshire,
at Chatsworth. The vigour of his body remained
unimpaired. He continued to play tennis until he
was nearly eighty. In the country, for want of a
tennis court, he would walk " up hill and downe-
hill in the parks, till he was in a great sweat, and then
give the servant some money to rubbe him." His
days were regular. He would rise at seven, take a
little bread and butter, and meditate until ten.
" He walked much and contemplated, and he had in
the head of his staffe a pen and inke-horn, carried
alwayes a note-book in his pocket, and as soon as a
thought darted, he presently entered it into his

booke, or otherwise he might perhaps have lost it."
He was suspicious of doctors, shy of medicines, and
had his own theories on matters of health. " He was
wont to say that he would rather have the advice, or
take physique from an experienced old woman, that
had been at many sick people's bed-sides, than from
the learnedest but unexperienced physitian."

He calculated that he had been drunk one hundred
times, which, as Aubrey comments, was not very
often, considering his longevity. After reaching the
grand climacteric he was very abstemious at the table,
choosing fish rather than flesh, especially " whitings "
if he could come by them. It was the custom of this
grand old man, " brimfull of prodigious impieties,"
to sing himself to sleep with " prick songs," books of
which he always kept in his chamber for the purpose.
" He did beleeve it did his lunges good, and conduced
much to prolong his life." Possibly we may trace
to this peculiar custom the rumour that he was afraid
to lie alone at night because of ghosts, a rumour
that he stoutly denied, characteristically declaring
" that he was not afrayd of *sprights*, but afrayd of
being knockt on the head for five or ten pounds,
which rogues might think he had in his chamber."

He was six foot and over, and held himself to
the end very upright. In the winter he dressed in a
black velvet coat lined with fur, and always wore
boots of Spanish leather " laced or tyed along the
sides with black ribbons." The skin of his face was
soft, " of that kind which my Lord Chancellor Bacon

in his *History of Life and Death* calles a goose-skin."
He never affected to look like a philosopher : " He
desired not the reputation of his wisdom to be taken
from the cutt of his beard." His whiskers, yellowish
red in colour, were inclined to turn up—" a signe of a
brisque witt." He was very bald, and yet within
doors would always sit bareheaded and never catch
cold, though he was often troubled to keep the
" flies from pitching on the baldness." Till his
dying day he spoke with a Wiltshire accent, and was
obstinate to describe himself as Thomas Hobbes of
Malmesbury. The Herald's office would have
supplied him with a coat of arms, but he refused it—
" The most worthy men have been rock't in mean
cradles." At the age of eighty-six, " to take off my
adversaries from showing their folly upon my more
serious writings," he translated the Iliad and the
Odyssey. It is difficult to believe that the meeting
between Hector and Andromache has ever been
rendered into English with more grace :—

> " Now Hector met her with their little boy
> That in the nurse's arms was carried,
> And like a star upon her bosom lay
> His beautiful and shining golden head."

He would often say that he would " revisit in his
dreams " those early happy days of his life when he
first entered the service of the Devonshire house-
hold; but we are not without evidence that he never
wholly relinquished his attachment to the present
hour of his experience. Aubrey says in connection

with Hobbes, " It is not consistent with an harmonical
soul to be a woman hater."   We know that Hobbes
left one natural daughter, whom he provided for in
his will, and it is clear that even at ninety he remained
susceptible to the charms of women, his hazel eye
continuing to shine when delighted as if " it had a
live bright coal in it."   What little lady of fashion
was it that came tripping between the quincunxes
on the Chatsworth lawns bringing romance to the
hours of the old pensioner, who, as long ago as Queen
Elizabeth's reign, had " turned Euripde's Medea out
of Greeke into Latin Iambiques "—a baggage of
quality destined perhaps under a gilded candelabra
in some Queen Anne dancing gallery to idle, frivolous
and sedate, with patched flashing cheeks, after her
lover?   None knew better than the " great clerk,"
as his adversaries used sarcastically to call him, that
no angels have ever existed " except those in
petticoats," and how engaging it is to think that this
love poem, so light and so living, came from the
charmed imagination of so ancient a poet.

> " Tho' I am now past ninety, and too old
> T' expect preferment in the Court of Cupid
> And many winters make mee ev'n so cold
> I am become almost all over stupid.
>
> Yet I can love and have a mistresse too,
> As fair as can be and as wise as fair ;
> And yet not proud ; nor anything will doe
> To make me of her favour to despair.
>
> To tell you who she is were very bold ;
> But if i' th' character your selfe you find
> Thinke not the man a fool tho he be old
> Who loves in body fair a fairer mind."

The summer of his ninety-third year arrives, and
he informs his publisher that he is writing " somewhat to print in English." However, the stoutest
oak tree of the forest must fall to the ground at the
last. In November the Earl of Devonshire planned
to move with his family to his Hardwick estate.
Hobbes could not support the prospect of being left
behind, and, sick though he was, his benevolent
patron had a feather-bed placed in one of his coaches,
and it was upon this truly Roman litter that the old
man was carried towards the particular " hole "
prepared for him by fate " to creep out of the world
at." He died on December 4, 1679. " He was
put into a woollen shroud." His coffin, covered
with a white sheet and with a black hearse-cloth
over all, was carried on men's shoulders " a little
mile " to Hault Hucknall church. The mourners
were very handsomely entertained with funeral
bake-meats and wine " burned and raw." He was
buried near to the third Earl's grandmother
(Hobbes's first patroness), " close adjoining to the
rail of the monument." These words are to be read
in the inscription : *Vir probus et fama eruditionis
forisque bene cognitus.* The exact resting-place of his
bones is marked by a black marble slab—" the true
philosopher's stone," as one of his witty friends
wrote. He left in his will over a thousand pounds,
which was more than expected, " considering his
charity." He was a man esteemed by both rich
and poor. They appreciated his company for his

" pleasant facetiousness " and good temper, and loved him for his " honesty " and for " the sweetness of his nature." He was ever against " too hasty concluding," and in appearance is said to have resembled his friend Galileo, the first great scientist— " both were chearfull and melancholique-sanguine; and both had a consimilitee of fate, to be hated and persecuted by the ecclesiastiques."

Free men are justified in regarding Hobbes as a weather-worn signpost still able to indicate their correct road. " Reason is the pace; encrease of science the way, and the benefit of mankind the end." No other English philosopher, not even Bacon himself, is more worthy of immortal remembrance than is this " great Columbus of the golden land of new philosophies."